Praise for *UNIFIED: Cosmos, Life, Purpose*

UNIFIED is an outstanding contribution toward the pursuit of an age-old and indeed perennial quest: to understand the world in which we live, of which we are a part, and with which we can also interact. The author leads us to querying the most authentic of all possible sources: not the human mind, even of a genius, but the cosmos itself — more exactly, the Unified Information Field which is how the cosmos presents itself to humans.

If you ever wondered what there is "really" behind the phenomena that meets your eye - and beyond even the most abstruse/advanced scientific theory — this is your book. It gives you answers that no human could give by himself or herself — because these answers come not from a human, but <u>through</u> a human - one who is communicating with The Source. Is that credible? Read the book, and judge for yourself. It will be a notable experience that will impact on all you have held real and true in the world.

Ervin Laszlo, author of *Reconnecting to the Source* & *Science and the Akashic Field*

***

UNIFIED is a unique synthesis of insights drawn from contemporary science with information channeled not from a single being but from a larger unified field of awareness. The result is a deep re-visioning of human existence with a special focus on the critical transition humanity has entered. Fascinating reading at the crossroads with a keen eye for what is needed in the years ahead.

Chris Bache, author of *LSD and the Mind of the Universe*

UNIFIED

COSMOS, LIFE, PURPOSE

ALSO BY KINGSLEY L. DENNIS

Hijacking Reality: The Reprogramming & Reorganization of Human Life

Healing the Wounded Mind: Mass Psychosis in the Modern World & The Search for Self

The Modern Seeker: A Perennial Psychology for Contemporary Times

The Sacred Revival: Magic, Myth & the New Human

Bardo Times: hyperreality, high-velocity, simulation, automation, mutation - a hoax?

The Phoenix Generation: A New Era of Connection, Compassion and Consciousness

Dawn of the Akashic Age: New Consciousness, Quantum Resonance, and the Future of the World (co-authored with Ervin Laszlo)

Breaking the Spell: An Exploration of Human Perception

New Revolutions for a Small Planet: How the Coming Years Will Transform Our Lives & Minds

The Struggle for Your Mind: Conscious Evolution and the Battle to Control How We Think

New Consciousness for a New World

After the Car (co-authored with John Urry)

UNIFIED

COSMOS, LIFE, PURPOSE

Communicating with the
Unified Source Field

And How This Can Guide Our Lives

KINGSLEY L. DENNIS

(with Nicola Mortimer)

Beautiful Traitor Books

CONTENTS

Introduction

Why we become our own obstacle

Is it you or I,
this reality in the eye?
Beware, beware
of the word "two"!

Al-Hallaj

We have not heeded Al-Hallaj's warning – we have become two. That is, humanity has largely become splintered and disconnected from its original unity. We have come to a point where much of modern life exists within a polarized bubble. There is us, and then there is everything else that lies external to us – and between these two there is little, if no, connection. This has become the modern mantra, and it is applied across the board to most aspects of our lives – to Nature and the environment; personal relations; other living creatures; events and circumstances; and even to those we refer to as our 'gods.' In short, the contemporary worldview is one of incredible isolation. We may consider that modern life is globally connected like never before, and we would be correct in this thinking – up to a point. As a species upon this planet we have become interconnected to an unparalleled degree. Our communications spread around the world in less than seconds; news is shared across cultures and languages; and algorithms trade economies in split seconds. The majority of people now receive and react to incoming messages on their smartphones and devices almost instantly. And yet, despite all this – and amidst all this – we are separated as a species like never before. Yet this separation is an internal one. We have become separated not only from ourselves, from our *sense* of self, but also from our contact with the larger cosmos – our sense of *origin*.

The dominant belief systems currently active on this planet also swing between polarities – again, the polarized bubble. On one hand we are largely servants to a creative god(s) figure that watch over us from a 'distance;' or we are an accidental anomaly striving to survive against the odds as we cling onto a lifeless rock hurtling in fast orbit through dead space. These beliefs – and they are just that, some unknown story to *believe* – are in need of being replaced by a new understanding.

That which is the new understanding requires time to be grounded and rooted because dominant beliefs, thinking patterns, and perspectives (our worldview) has been engrained in us for so long. Yet once we can begin to change our views, we will find that a great many unexpected new life situations will suddenly appear. Life takes on a new meaning with every shift in our perspectives. It can be like a new breath of fresh air. Old, habitual comments that once fitted our situations and circumstances will no longer apply or seem adequate. A new rethinking will be required. Human thinking is what drives our cultures, societies, and our overall civilizational progress. Once this becomes redundant, and then stagnant, so too does our progress stall. There are moments, epochs in the human evolutionary journey, when significant shifts in consciousness, understanding, and knowledge are required. We are living within one of these monumental transition periods right now. And what is more, we have become our very own obstacle.

It is said that when people actively try to guess a card or dice, they will make so many mistakes that it becomes statistically impossible for them to be wrong so many times. And yet why is this so? What has been shown by psychologists is that people are in fact guessing right more of the time, but some 'inner censor' prevents them from admitting it, and actually blocks this so that they guess wrong. We have an in-built detector that instead of proving us right is actually working to positively prove us wrong! A part of the human personality actively seeks to protect a person's existing ways of thought – their status quo and sense of familiarity – in order not to push the boundaries beyond their conditioning, or social programming. Unknown to many of us, this creates a silent conflict within whereby half of the person (the instinctual 'gut feeling') knows the truth and wants it; and the other half blocks the acceptance of this fact, since it is dedicated to maintaining the status quo (the 'way it's always been').

If a person were to admit the truth to themselves, they would be facing the unknown, and this scares many people whether they openly admit it or not. The human personality – an aggregation of years of social conditioning – fears change; or, at the very least, of stepping away from the comforting world of the familiar. Why – what would happen? Maybe, just maybe, a person would become motivated by something else – new ideas, creative possibilities, new perspectives, and new insights that may be closer to the truth than the bundle of the 'familiar' that they have carried around for so long.

Here is an illustrative tale. A wise man was once asked who had guided him upon his path to wisdom. The wise man answered: a dog. Then he related the following story:

> One day I a dog almost dead with thirst, although standing by the water's edge. Every time the dog looked at his reflection in the water, he became frightened, and withdrew, because he thought it was another dog.

> Finally, such was this dog's thirst, and necessity, that he threw away his fear and leapt into the water. At this, the 'other dog' disappeared.

The dog found that the obstacle, which was himself, was the real barrier between him and what he sought.

In this same way, my own obstacle vanished when I knew that it was what I took to be my own self that was the blockage. And so, my path to wisdom was first shown to me by the behaviour of a dog.

Our beliefs become our own fears too. What we take to be our ideas, our thoughts, and our opinions, can become the very same things that act as impediments to greater understanding and realization. And the further we step *outside* of ourselves, the further we stray from our own internal mechanisms of truth – our gut instinct.

Part of the problem associated with our current polarized bubble is that we have outsourced our sense of dependency onto external structures and institutions. And yet so many of our current structures and institutions are now found lacking – our religious bodies, orthodox science, and our socio-political establishments, to name a few. If our source of dependency is placed upon such external structures, then we naturally feel undermined, vulnerable, and sometimes helpless when those very same structures are shown to be failing us. Such feelings of helplessness and vulnerability are an indication of our own loss of wholeness – of our separation from the greater cosmic field of life and meaning. It shows that so many of us have cut our umbilical cord from the greater source of a unified, integral whole. In other words, we are no longer self-sustainable.

Our sustainability is now largely not through internal connections but rather through external ones. To become self-sustainable individuals, we must realize that we have everything we need exactly where we are – exactly because we are simultaneously connected to everything else. And this does not mean only our external social and cultural structures but to the whole cosmic intelligence field. And it is exactly this point that is going to stretch many people's pre-conditioned concepts.

What this book offers the reader is a completely new understanding of life, the universe, and everything. The reader is going to experience a whole new perspective on life in the cosmos through reading this book. This can either change everything in your life; or, your 'inner censor' will prevent you from admitting it and block you – just like guessing wrong in cards or dice. What you are going to read within these pages is likely to either amaze you or infuriate you. The choice is going to be yours. What this book is going to show is that not only is there a conscious, unified field of energy that is the Source of Everything – but that this unified field actively speaks through us constantly. And we are going to be having a conversation with it – a conversation with ourselves.

As I've said, there is little doubt that the premise of this book will challenge many readers. Yet the fact that you have this book in your hands suggests that initial steps have already been made. As the reader will soon find out, *unification* is a positive path – a nurturing way back to ourselves through the distortions and distractions of the modern world. It is no less than a homecoming. And I am not alone in feeling that the time is now ripe, even over-ripe, for a change to come along. It no longer serves the human race to be loosely stuck between the polarities of 'there is an almighty god – and take your pick of the contenders' and 'life is an accident – it's a bummer but get used to it.' Our modes of understanding, and thus our parameters of thinking, have begun to shift – and about time too. The cracks in the dominant paradigms of thought are now showing through.

In the modern world, people are beginning to understand, outside of religious terminology, the concept of the absolute one Reality. Science is now confirming what mystics and sages have said for centuries. The quantum sciences have validated that there exists an underlying quantum field – sometimes referred to as the quantum vacuum, plenum, matrix, or even the akashic field. From this underlying collective field manifests all materiality (matter-reality). That is, all material existence is fundamentally and inextricably interconnected; and all life is connected to the same underlying field. Further, that this underlying 'unified' field is not only energetic but also conscious. Not everyone agrees on this point - yet. However, a number of scientists have now agreed that the underlying energetic field of all existence is pure consciousness, as I show in the early chapters.

According to the ancient Vedic understanding - All is Brahman. There is nothing that is not Brahman, for outside Brahman nothing exists – because all is Brahman – the ancient. As the Indian sage Sri Aurobindo once put it, in answer to a question – 'Brahman, sir, is the name given by Indian philosophy since the beginning of time to the one Reality, eternal and infinite, which is the Self, the Divine, the All, the more than All…In fact, sir, you are Brahman.' In this understanding, there is no separation between that which we may call 'god' on the one hand, and all manifestation and creation on the other.

The idea of a deity somewhere 'above' us, seated on a throne, and observing all that has been created, has now become an outdated concept. As the reader shall soon see, many pre-existing concepts, beliefs, and ideas of separation are part of humanity's 'splintered mind.' Within a unified mind, everything is in communication – or communion – with itself. After all, why shouldn't we humans, as the physical-spiritful beings that we are, be able to communicate with the Unified Source from which we manifested forth?

This book is organized in three parts. In Part One - *What is Reality?* - I present the latest cutting-edge understandings from modern science. Here I explain how matter-reality manifests from an intelligent cosmic field that itself is an expression of the Unified Source Field. I then further outline how this provides for a new model of consciousness that operates largely external to our brains/bodies. This new model of consciousness will allow the reader to better appreciate the understanding of how life exists within collective fields. I also examine how quantum field resonance operates within the human body that connects us to larger energetic fields. From this perspective, I offer a new worldview that brings in more wonder and enchantment into a grand picture of reality. In the final chapter of Part One, I offer some alternative vistas from other explorers who have entered and communed with the mind of the cosmos.

Then in Part Two – *The Way Back Home: The ABE Communications* – I introduce a series of questions and answers taken from communications with the Unified Source Field. These topics range from understanding what it is and *how* we can communicate with it: to issues of bodily health, the human mind and body; human society & culture; our technologies; to humanity and our future. These communications have been provided through a lady called Nicola Mortimer. Nicola has been communicating with this unified field for most of her adult life. In Part Two I introduce Nicola further, discussing how Nicola engages with the unified field (which has given the moniker of ABE) and how the both of us established an on-going series of communications. Part Two is thus a collaborative work with what we have come to call our triad – Nicola, myself, and ABE. Just how the unified field came to give itself the name of ABE will be outlined when we get there. I also explain the distinct style and manner of the stream-of-consciousness that is received from ABE. What I come to suggest is that the reader considers the following Source Field communications in this book as a conversation between ourselves.

In fact, we did pose this as a question:

If our consciousnesses are intertwined, then is it possible that you know our questions before we ask them? It is like having a conversation between ourselves.

To which came the reply:

> One could say that yes, for that is how we would see it. Like the whole universe is mad, talking to oneself...the whole universe talking to itself to be able to know itself. These things set in motion as little pointers to wake you up like alarm clocks dotted all about the universe.

Part Three - *Re-Connecting to Our Future* – offers an analysis and reflection upon the implications of the ABE communications. I explore what it means to be connected within a unified and intelligent cosmic field and how this understanding may impact our lives. Certainly, this knowledge will come to have great impact upon our perceptions as a collective human species. I also deal with the possibilities that humanity is passing through a period of collective turbulence – a 'Dark Night of the Soul' – as a necessary part of our evolutionary transition. Finally, I explore the implications of purpose and meaning upon human life if we acknowledge that all existence is a manifestation from the conscious Unified Source

Field. What are our responsibilities? How will this impact our human future? How can this enrich our lives? I come to these major questions in the final chapter.

For now, intrepid reader, let us venture forth without our blinkers, our rigid belief systems, and our socially instilled opinions. Just for the moment, for the duration of reading this book, let's just drop all this baggage and just *allow* – allow the conversations to take you to new places. You may never be the same again…

PART ONE

What is Reality?

Chapter One

Our Quest for Meaning

The most beautiful experience we can have is the mysterious. It is the fundamental emotion that stands at the cradle of true art and true science. Whoever does not know it and can no longer wonder and stand rapt in awe, is as good as dead, and his eyes are dimmed.

Albert Einstein

Humanity has lived with a particular worldview for so long now that it is becoming difficult, extremely difficult, to give it up. It is a worldview that has brought our species to the cusp of being a hugely interconnected planetary society with great resilience. It has created a shared vision of immense capability and has established nations and complex societies that have developed a range of innovations, technological mastery, and material expansion beyond the hopes and dreams of our human ancestors. And yet, strangely enough, at the very end of it all it has left humanity feeling deeply estranged.

As a collective social group, we have grown estranged from ourselves, from each other, from our natural environment, and from the greater cosmic reality in which we live and breathe. We feel alone amongst the stars.

In previous epochs humanity had its connection with its god(s) to provide meaning, security, and a sense of destiny or fate. As a whole, humanity more or less shared a range of common beliefs in something greater than itself, something 'beyond,' that was in some way or form watching over, or watching out, for our goodwill. Immense monuments, sacred sites, religious edifices, and other such awe-inspiring structures were built with great fortitude and faith to attest to these beliefs. Humanity existed for millennia through acts of faith. Even though we walked the earth's byways physically alone, somehow deep within our hearts we felt a form of contact. We once adored Nature because of this and lived our lives under the protective umbrella of her seasons. Our ancestors rose to her sounds and slept to the setting of her light. And now?

Now, humanity rises daily to the grind of fragmented lives. Lives splintered into digitized time-slots, monitored by constant beeps, surveyed by artificial eyes, manoeuvred into positions by seen and unseen hands of power, fed by food-on-credit, and programmed by a morass of dumbed-down information. Somewhere along the way, we got terribly lost. Not only did we lose our sense of self – we also lost our greater sense of being cosmic players in a wondrous game of life.

Once upon a time we had a direct line with home. We knew we were on the receiving end of an on-going conversation. When we looked up into the night sky and saw the sparkle of stars, we were awed and enchanted. We recognized the grace, the wonder, and the excitement of the unknown. Everything came alive with possibility. That possibility is still there. It never went away. Only that so many people closed their eyes – their hearts and minds – and closed the connection. Or life's uncertain, and sometimes cruel, circumstances closed the connection for them. Yet there remains an enchanted world out there, and it beckons, awaiting for humanity to respond to its call. Underlying all life is the quest for meaning.

As human beings we desire, long for – *need* – a sense of meaning and purpose in our lives. An enchanted, immersive cosmos can give that sense of belonging. Yet somewhere along the way we lost the sense of communion. In our past, we once felt and shared a common destiny with the environment - both terrestrial and cosmic - and this encouraged a mode of 'direct participation.' There was a time when our ancestors did not stand away from life but instead, they participated directly in its enchantment. This merger between being and environment established a psychic wholeness in the human being. Our far ancestors were not estranged from the world in the way that modern humanity has become. In the last few centuries especially, humankind has chosen to adopt a worldview that encouraged it to become masters of its environment. Material hunger and greed became dominant principles that were lauded and praised and given priority. Humanity became a new type of hunter and chased after a different type of prey. Modern life eventually encouraged a predatory form of living that not only has resulted in extreme forms of inequality, poverty, and domination; more importantly perhaps, it has resulted in the modern human throwing itself out of its own mystery and abandoning the realm of enchantment.

Modern scientific, rational consciousness has become an alienated form of consciousness, afraid of its own participation. It views the world from the position of an uninterested observer, or as an uninvited guest. It sees a world of objects that move in mechanical motion. This alienated consciousness has substituted the enchantment and mystery with that of the artificial. The participatory cosmos where the human 'being and belonging' once felt at home soon became corrupted with the contagion of the modern human mind. Yet this is not how things are - it is only the latest picture of how things *seem to us*. We have been forced to construct our own meanings about a world we have let slip from our grasp. In other words, humanity has disenchanted itself from a living cosmos. Until now, that's the way it's become.

The Way We Have Been

Things are going to change – they will *have* to change. We need to remove ourselves from a modern landscape that is now more about administration than adventure. A landscape that strives for control rather than compassion. People are being programmed to become entangled into a system that does not have their welfare at heart. Rather than disentangling ourselves, we are more and more buying *into* the system, and merging with its inanimate ideology. The easy acquisition of things is no substitute for contentment. The inner psychological landscape of so many people has become infected with a form of world weariness, and it is spreading like a contagion. This is no surprise considering that the dominant lens which we have looked out at the world around us, and at the cosmos, has been one of a dull disenchantment. Life became defined as one grand accident - a colossal conglomeration of chance and chaos. That was just how life came to be ordained.

The modern history of the West has been about the removal of mystery and magic from the world. The western consciousness came to define itself by its very removal from the world 'beyond.' It is a consciousness predicated on the belief of linear progress that is mechanical, and without conscious direction. Whether we call our present age the modern or post-modern, the underlying current is the same. Many of us seem to be spending our lives not in fear of what may happen to us, but in fear that nothing will happen. This malaise has, for many, been turned into an expression of anger and harm, both to self and to others. It is ironic that the very institutions of learning and meaning have recently (in the US predominantly) become the very sites of violence, terror, and meaningless murder. This psychic space, where reality and unreality are in conflict, is a response to our dominant state of consciousness. Until now, this dominant worldview has largely been constructed from the scientific-rational perspective. Yet we have now entered a period of deep transition. During such times of change, the impulse for meaning and significance becomes a more prominent and necessary urge. In such moments of social-cultural transformation, when bases of knowledge and constructions of reality are questioned, the need to seek meaning within the self grows stronger in the individual.

The scientific-rational consciousness contains its own in-built limitations; namely, the separation and disenchantment of the living cosmos. This 'modern' so-called scientific paradigm, like the religious paradigm of the 17th century, now finds itself unable to be maintained. This is how things unfold; one set of structures, systems, viewpoints, are eventually outmoded and, through necessity (amongst other factors) get replaced, or rather updated, by a new set. This new set then defines the dominant consciousness for the new era. New values too come to the fore to represent the emergent expression of consciousness. In such transitional times there is urgency, opportunity, and an interior push to re-connect with a sense of meaning, both personal and cosmic. In other words, there is a fundamental need to understand one's 'self' and its place in the larger scheme of things. The instability in the world at this time is further indication for the need to find the roots that connect humanity with a more permanent stream of knowledge and meaning. This is precisely the theme of this book. What I present in Part Two is a way of re-connecting with the Source of ourselves – to begin a communication with the collective consciousness field from which our localised point of consciousness manifests. This re-connecting can show each person a way back home – forward to a new beginning

In the beginning...

In the beginning, when conscious reflective thought arose within humanity, all our mental enquiries were unified into a single stream that became a sacred quest – to connect with and *to know* our Source. Philosophy and science too were once on the same endeavour to seek and understand humanity's origins. These early human enquiries had a metaphysical thirst. The human spirit longed to seek beyond the rhythm of the stars and the suns. Our ancestors watched and tracked the cycles of day and night - the great arc of star-sprinkled skies - and the heavenly revolutions. From this they calculated a measurement of time, mathematics, and reason. And with these tools they expanded the mind's reach to traverse the possibilities of life, with its whys and wherefores, endlessly searching once again for the original stream of humanity's origins. It is the spirit that seeks, that calls out, wishing to know and be known. Finally, it was human society that came to clothe and hide the spirit under many layers of cultural conditioning. And yet, the soul of humanity – the soul of the world – has never ceased from seeking. As T.S. Eliot famously wrote: '*We shall not cease from exploration, and the end of all our exploring will be to arrive where we started and know the place for the first time.*'

For thousands of years, in various cultures across the globe from the ancient Egyptians to Mesoamerica, divination, myth, ritual, and direct intervention with the gods all formed part of the holistic human experience. Dealings with phenomena beyond materiality informed the psychological and spiritual development of the human being. Such mythology constituted a healthy and integral part of human consciousness. Such a 'pre-modern' consciousness was also one where the ego was kept in check by the presence of powerful transcendental forces that were believed to play a permanent part in human lives. Such transcendental powers were perceived as being the real players behind human existence. And such powers were not only acting upon the human being externally but also formed a part of their interior psyche. As such, aspects of the individual – their thoughts, feelings, desires, and intentions – were not as strongly developed and manifested as they are today. In those ancient times, the human was not considered apart from such powers, energies, or consequences in the way that the modern individual believes today. This integration within the cosmological order created a natural sense of meaning and participation.

Yet by the first century AD, the essayist Plutarch was asking 'Why is it that the gods are no longer speaking to us?' By that time there had been a steep decline in the prestige of the Oracles and the divination that was once held so prominent in Greek culture. However, a great majority of people still believed that their lives, both internal and external, were influenced by forces beyond them, and which also infused their soul. For millennia, the boundaries between 'inner' and 'outer,' between 'subjective' and 'objective,' had become blurred; one did not know where to place the dividing lines, if indeed there were any. The external world of nature and the inner world of the human psyche were inextricably merged, and both were spiritualized in their own ways. Yet soon, the seemingly inevitable process of separation would have its effect. It began by a loosening of this mergence until rather than being inextricably bound, the realms became seen as attached through forms of 'correspondence.'

The medieval world – coming after the pre-modern (or antiquity), and before the modern period – formed a belief in the notion of *correspondence*. In this context, correspondence implied that things of the world had relations of 'sympathy' - a form of magical action at a distance - between them. Just as people attract one another, minerals attract minerals, and oil repels water, etc, so too do sympathies exist between elements of the cosmos and the earth. We can see this being played out in the famous Hermetic axiom of 'as above, so below' set of relationships. Resemblance and sympathy were known aspects in the medieval mindset, although the church orders worked hard to expel them on charges of heresy. Many of these practices were termed as *occult* and driven underground.

It was not long before the modernizing mindset wished to take a step back and to see elements in their isolation, and not to confuse the relation of things. Those 'archaic minds' that could not accept the consensus thinking of separated, lifeless elements were soon deemed mad, or paranoiac. A famous example in literature appears in Cervante's *Don Quixote* when his character sees the windmills as giants – in his world such things found their own correspondences and relations that to a modern mind 'do not compute,' as we say. Where there was no consensus programming, the social establishment saw this as a threat. Or rather, in the medieval world it was a threat to the religious order. The understanding of *correspondences* eventually went into survival mode and slipped below the external skin of everyday medieval life. As a consequence, the Middle Ages grew stagnant as there was little movement in creative vision, myth, and the innovative ideas that propel cultures ever forward. The great separation of human consciousness began in earnest.

The Great Separation

Over the centuries human consciousness has undergone a 'dis-coupling' from the world around it; a distancing that has been referred to as *disgodding* from nature.[1] This refers to a break away from an integral relationship with the environment, and creating a distance between the human being and everything else. In short, humanity succeeded in taking itself 'out of the picture' by creating a new world picture for itself. The rejection of the earlier participatory consciousness – often referred to as animism – owed a debt to the dominance of monotheistic religion. It also was influenced by the rationalistic side of Greek thought and philosophy

. . . .
1   A phrase from Friedrich Schiller

that aimed to push aside instinct in favour of observation and experimentation.

Early monotheistic religion viewed participatory consciousness as sin, whilst rational Hellenistic thought considered it a pathology of the mind. Both served to expunge it from the human experience and to usher in a dis-coupled consciousness that has resulted in the current mode of a 'splintered consciousness.' This process did not occur overnight, and fragments of participatory consciousness continued down the ages until it met its final demise in the 17th Century's Scientific Revolution.

The Scientific Revolution of 17th Century Western Europe established a new way of perceiving reality. An important aspect of this shift was a change from quality to quantity - from the 'why' of things to the 'how.' The cosmos, once viewed as alive and with purpose, now became inert - a mechanical moratorium of meaningless matter. Nature became a thing to be probed and controlled, stepped back from and observed, rather than as something to merge and participate with. This was the time of Francis Bacon and the birth of modern empiricism and the need for rational enquiry and inductive reasoning. Metaphysical notions were relegated to romantic fantasies, as direct manipulation of the environment became the principal tool. A deliberate commodity management of the world replaced the enchanted wonder of an immersive and magical experience. Humanity had made a full degree turn from participant (early humankind), to passive observers (Religious Revolution), to material manipulators (Scientific Revolution). The ideas of the Scientific Revolution were put fully into play during the western Industrial Revolutions.

The collapse of the feudal economy and the rise of capitalism as a major force profoundly altered social relations in modern Europe and created a context for applying the tools of the Scientific Revolution. Quantification and control would not have had its place in a medieval world yet was ideally suited to the rise of industrial capitalism. Modern science has proved itself to be ideally suited to a world of capital accumulation as both ideologies share a similar mentality and worldview.

The medieval worldview had its own sense of completeness, where divine principle ordered the movement, positions, and purpose of all life in the heavens, as above and below. The world thus became endowed with meaning, albeit its own interpretation of meaning. The notion of a God was pivotal at this time as it gave people a foundation of faith upon which to rely on during their difficult lives. The individual in medieval times had meaning allotted to them, despite it being from an external authority. The individual of the scientific-rational era had to search through the newly declared inert environment to seek a sense of significance. It was a totally different world. The scientific mind could give out facts and data, but it fell short in providing genuine meaning. A significant psychological shift had occurred that would deeply affect humankind.

The Loss of Meaning

This latest psychological shift dramatically affected the individual. The closed medieval world - with its feudal structure, country folk, religious order, and close networks - nevertheless provided a psychologically safe and secure environment with its known enclosure. The advent of the scientific-rational-capitalist era changed all this when it threw the individual mind into a brutal world of merciless mechanism, management, and meaningless industrial-urban landscapes. The individual of the new modern Europe lost their purposeful footing in the race for nationalist expansion.

Nationalist expansion also meant naval expansion, as the old world opened up to the new. Science helped in creating instruments and methods for naval navigation, as well as for colonial conquest. Expansion of territory meant that the closed medieval European world was left behind in the enviable pursuit of progress. Long-distance trading saw a revolution in commerce that crushed local artisan and barter trade. The mercantile class gradually replaced the guild-master and journeyman, personal trade relationships broke down, and credit systems arose to fill the demand. It was a tremendous shift that psychologically altered the mentality, perception, and worldview of the modern human and the peoples they had contact with.

The ecumenical order of the medieval world had been replaced by a new economic order. The logic and rationality of this was that when salvation and pardon could be bought by money, those with money had salvation. Economy became the 'divine' goal for the new era of progress. Financial calculation became the new road to comprehending the once creative cosmos. A new modern West was being constructed that viewed progress separate from the meaning and metaphysical significance of the individual. With the cosmos as now something functioning within concrete mechanical laws, the latest pioneers of humankind could continue unabated with their goals of conquest and competition. A new type of consciousness had seated itself at the forefront of human social development. The late 17th and early 18th centuries did their best to discard, disprove, and remove the inner psychic landscape of the western individual. The inner reality of the human did not adhere to the incoming programs of capitalist commerce and industrial mechanization, expansion, and management.

Despite the seemingly outward appearance of stability, human civilization has been in a state of inward instability and crisis for several centuries. The modern schismatic consciousness that has been embraced as 'normal' has led to the present state of world volatility. It is not about thinking straight, as we have been led to believe, but rather about thinking relational. The Cartesian-Newtonian paradigm, which split the world into parts and mechanized their relations, ruptured the necessary harmony between all things. We have been living since within a splintered consciousness that has led humanity astray from its sense of origin.

Historians will eventually look back on this phase of human civilization and see it as a relic. It will be viewed as a period of ahistorical time that created rapid industrial expansion and scientific knowledge whilst simultaneously creating a rupture within human consciousness. The last few centuries were a single evolutionary episode that ran its course. In anthropological terms it was a mere blink of an eye. And in that blink humanity brought itself to the brink of collapse. Yet at the last step, it seems, humankind may very well pull itself back upon the path. Within the deepest hearts of humanity, the urge for a transpersonal connection and communion may once again be rising.

A Search for Source

The search for meaning has never been more urgent than it is now. As I show in the coming chapters, the latest findings from the world of science, of quantum physics and biology, are aligning with ancient metaphysical and mystical knowledge. The living cosmos is coming back into view. And with it arises an understanding of the primacy of consciousness over matter. The inner landscape of humanity is once again merging into communion and contact with the cosmic intelligence field. Our innate species longing is for unification. We naturally need to sense an integral empathy of relations, contact, and meaning. This is the sacred reality that needs to be re-installed and rebooted into humanity's collective consciousness. This is, for each person, the way back home.

First though, we must shift into a new mode of consciousness. This begins by re-examining our view of the cosmos. I now turn to this.

Chapter Two
A New View of the Cosmos

*'Stories emphasize the operations of divine immanence
in the world.'*

Jonathan Black

In the beginning...there were many myths of how
the cosmos came into existence. Many of the great
spiritual traditions told of how the material world
came into being out of a nameless domain. Some
traditions have spoken of the 'cosmic egg' from
which form emerged; or, as in the Old Testament,
out of the dark and formless deep where the spirit of
God moved. The Hindu spiritual traditions of India
speak of an underlying reality that is Brahman – a
reality that is eternal and eternally unchanging. In
this cosmology, the world of space and time that we
are familiar with is known as *lila,* which describes
our physical world as the playground of unceasing
creative play within Brahman. The ancient Hindu
Vedic rishis told that the essence of all things in the
material world belonged to *Akasha.* A Sanskrit term,
Akasha refers to the fifth element of the cosmos,

beyond air (*vata*), fire (*agni*), water (*jal*), and earth (*prithivi*). The concept of Akasha is similar to the later western notions of *aether* – a space field that contains all the elements within itself. In the late 6th century BC Pythagoras spoke of the 'aether' as the fifth element of the world, in addition to earth, air, fire and water. In modern terminology, there are similarities with the notion of the underlying quantum vacuum (or plenum, matrix) that is described as the energetic sea of the cosmos from which matter-reality manifests. The Akasha/aether/quantum matrix has been recognized by various traditions as the cosmic energy domain from which everything has emerged, and into which everything will ultimately return.

Western streams of philosophic thought also speak of a domain beyond space and time. According to Plato, there was a realm of Forms and Ideas – a domain of Pure Forms – beyond our space and time, and that our material world is only an image or copy of this real, pure world beyond. This *pure realm* was also spoken of by other Hellenic philosophers: Pythagoras referred to it as *Kosmos*, and Plotinus as *The One*. Perhaps the most famous illustration of Plato's thinking is his allegory of The Cave. In this allegory Plato describes a group of people who have lived all their lives chained up and facing the wall of a cave. All they can see is the blank cave wall that lies in front of them. The opening of the cave is behind them, and the light that enters casts shadows on the far wall of the cave. Upon this wall, day after day, the chained people watch shadows move across as they cannot turn around and see the 'real' objects that pass behind them. A familiar depiction of this allegory is seen below:

Thus, they view these shadows as their reality and ascribe forms, reason, and life to them. This is the illusion – the shadows from beyond – that we ascribe as our 'reality' and give meaning to.

Similarly, the Chinese sage Lao-Tze (or Laozi) spoke of all things originating in the Tao/ Dao as the unseen root of all material things. The Tao is both the originator (the source) of all things, and the destination to which all things eventually return. It is the unobservable and nameless no-space, no-time, no-form essence that our words fail.

These various cosmological philosophies indicate that there is an active feedback relationship between the physical world of phenomena and the 'unseen' worlds – the domain of Pure Forms, *Kosmos*, *The One*, the Tao (the energetic realms of Source). The world of physical manifestation and its Source are engaged within mutual correspondences. It is this interplay that maintains the continual sustenance and the 'coming into being' of the material worlds. In this way, the material worlds are kept 'updated' as information is continually transmitted between realms. Many cosmological traditions agree that there is a continual correspondence maintained between the realm of matter-reality and its unseen Source dimension. As the 13th century Persian poet Rumi declared - 'Every moment the world is renewed, and we are unaware of its being renewed whilst it remains the same in appearance.'[2]

In this picture, the manifested physical universe remains in correspondence and continual 'update' with its energetic origin, or Source. Matter did not just appear 'out of nowhere' so to speak. This is contrary to the dominant scientific view that the material universe is clusters of matter surrounded by dead space. Yet even this perspective no longer holds up, according to scientific research itself. There is something wrong with the main narrative view of the cosmos.

The Cosmos is More Than We Know

It is now being revealed that contemporary physics has its limitations. The main consensus narrative is finding it tricky to come up with a solid explanation for the currently observed dynamics and features of the known universe. According to some of the existing calculations, many galaxies should be flying apart instead of rotating. Further, certain matter-formations within the universe should not be displaying movement, or even be existing, in the ways they have been observed. There are just too many so-called 'anomalies' for mainstream science to account for. So, how does the consensus narrative respond? Quite literally by inventing its own terms and theories to explain it all away.

In order to account for the registered anomalies, mainstream modern science has concluded that there must be some form of 'unknown substance' that is present within the universe. Furthermore, that there must also be some form of 'hidden' energy that also exists as part of the universe, and which explains its mysterious workings. And for this, modern science has come up with the 'theories' of 'dark matter' and 'dark energy' which, they postulate, must have a huge presence in the universe as they contribute massively to its structure and features. Why is everything so 'dark'? Quite simply, because science neither knows how to observe this 'hidden' phenomena nor how to adequately describe it – it is literally 'dark' to the scientists also. This unseen presence does not appear to interact with observable electromagnetic radiation. Because of this, it is 'invisible' to the electromagnetic spectrum and cannot be detected by available astronomical equipment. According to recent physics, about 68% of the universe is made up of what is now termed as dark energy, and 27% of dark matter. That makes only 5% of 'ordinary matter' that makes up the universe. What this tells us, very blatantly, is that our modern scientists, who are at the vanguard of discovery and understanding, are making a guess at 95% of the known universe. That has to be one very big guess in anyone's book.

It is now a good time to acknowledge that the universe is not filled with 'empty space,' which is a childish concept many of us grew up with. Rather, the entire universe is an energetic realm. And as I will show, this energetic realm that fills the known universe is a field consciousness that is constantly being 'in-formed' through information. First, I need to explain that if the observed universe is a constantly 'in-formed' field then we would expect the universe to manifest a marked degree of order. In other words, there should be evidence that the observable universe is not the result of some random, accidental play of forces. In fact, there are a surprisingly high number of 'coincidences' when it comes to the universe's numerical parameters.

One of the earliest to be discovered (by Arthur Eddington and Paul Dirac in the 1930s) was the ratio of the electric force to the gravitational force, which is approximately 1040 and, likewise, the ratio of the observable size of the universe to the size of elementary particles is about 1040. This is odd since the ratio of the size of the universe to the size of elementary particles should be changing as the universe is considered to be expanding. Dirac himself considered that the agreement of these ratios is more than a coincidence and is not temporary. There are also other numerical alignments, such as the ratio of elementary particles to the Planck-length (which is 1020) and the number of nucleons in the universe. These are huge numbers, and yet harmonic relations can be constructed from them.

Further, scientific observations have found that the cosmic microwave background radiation is dominated by a large peak followed by smaller harmonic peaks. Physicist Lee Smolin made a series of measurements based on this microwave background radiation and concluded that the measure of acceleration in the expansion of the galaxies corresponded to the actually observed value. Such 'coincidences' as these above have no explanation in mainstream cosmological physics. And not only is it the coincidences we should be surprised about - the physical processes that underlie the universe also appear to be incredibly fine-tuned.

It is not possible here to list all the staggeringly precise universal constants that 'just happened' to occur in order for life, as we know it, to arise in the universe. I shall, however, give several examples. One concerns the expansion rate of the early universe. If the expansion rate had been one-billionth less than it was, then the universe would have re-collapsed almost immediately. Similarly, if the expansion rate had been one-billionth more, it would have flown apart so fast that matter would not have been able to form. Another precise fine-tuning exists between the strength of the electromagnetic field relative to the gravitational field. If the difference had been other than it is, stable stars like our own sun would not have formed. Thus, the evolution of life on planets would not have been possible according to known laws. Yet another example is the difference between the mass of the neutron and the proton. If the mass of the neutron were not precisely twice the mass of the electron, then no substantial chemical reactions could take place. The known universe has a stable configuration, in terms of matter, precisely because the electric charges of electrons and protons have an accurate balance. In other words, the universe is incredibly fine-tuned beyond any possibility of chance. It could be said that we exist in a 'just-right' universe. According to the calculations of mathematical physicist Roger Penrose, the probability of coming across such a universe, fine-tuned to life by random selection, is 1 in $10^{10^{123}}$. There are no other words for it – the universe is spectacularly coherent beyond our comprehension. Its physical properties are also vastly different than science once theorized.

It was considered not only improbable but impossible that complex molecules could be synthesized near active stars. However, this has now been contradicted by the research of astrophysicists headed by Sun Kwok and Yong Zhang at the University of Hong Kong in 2011.[3] They found some 130 organic macromolecules (including glycine, an amino acid, and ethylene glycol) in the vicinity of active stars. Such compounds that were discovered are associated with the formation of the sugar molecules necessary for life. It appears that these compounds are produced in processes of stellar evolution. What these findings indicate is that life creation is not a rare or improbable occurrence in the universe, but part of the very evolution of its stars.

. . . .
3   Kwok, Sun. 2011. *Organic Matter in the Universe*. London: Wiley.

The examples cited here (and there are more) all indicate that the cosmos is far more coherently interconnected than orthodox science has considered – or even given credit for. As if on cue, cutting edge research has now shown that the universe is remarkably coherent. These relations, which statistically are far beyond randomness, reveal that coherence is the dominant driver ('attractor') in the universe. From quantum behavior to atoms, complex molecules, and living organisms, coherence appears to be an underlying purpose. There are, it seems, coherent relationships between events from one end of the universe to the other. The universe may not be a fully coherent system, yet coherence appears to be an innate universal orientation. This non-random nature of the universe suggests order above chance. Further, this drive toward emergent coherence is reflected throughout life on planet Earth and infuses human biological evolution.

A Coherent Cosmos

The intricate elements and processes that make up what we call life all exhibit forms of entanglement that, according to quantum science, show remarkable coherence. Physicists Eric Cornell, Wolfgang Ketterle, and Carl E. Wieman demonstrated that complex molecules, cells, and even living organisms exhibit quantum-type processes (and received the 1995 Nobel Prize for their discovery). What this shows is that complex organisms could not have evolved on this planet without some form of quantum coherence. The human body is one example, where each cell produces 10,000 bio-electro-chemical reactions every second; and where exists a constant flux of inter-reactions and processes connecting molecules, cells, organs, and fluids, throughout the brain, body and nervous system. Recent findings in biophysics have demonstrated that a form of quantum coherence operates within living biological systems through what is known as biological excitations and biophoton emission (see chapter four). What this means is that metabolic energy is stored as a form of electromechanical and electromagnetic excitations. Further, a quantum-level correlation in organisms is neither limited to the organisms themselves but also operates between organisms. That is, a complex ecology of organisms exists on this planet that is 'fine-tuned' via coherent fields establishing a biosphere that is interactive and participatory. Life on this planet is a *dance of coherence* between organisms and their environment.

Physical, chemical, and biological coherence leads ultimately to a degree of perception/ comprehension regarding types of relations and interconnectivity. The science philosopher Ervin Laszlo uses the term 'prehension' to describe this combination of perception and comprehension.[4] What this implies is an element of conscious interconnectivity between the various sub-parts of any system. That is, as parts of a given system become more complex and interdependent, there arises a greater degree of 'emergent perception'

· · · · · · · · · · · ·
4   Laszlo, Ervin, 2014. *The Self-Actualizing Cosmos: The Akasha Revolution in Science and Human Consciousness.* Rochester, VT: Inner Traditions.

regarding the relations of interconnectivity. In other words, coherence becomes a conscious purpose.

Coherent interconnection within and among systems (chemical, physical, and biological) has been the core attractor throughout all evolving systems within the material universe – including the universe itself. This trend toward more sensitive and stable coherence also serves as a drive toward emergent conscious interconnectivity. Behind this phenomenon, it has been hypothesized and to which I concur, exists a cosmic field of conscious intelligence.

According to a new model of the universe, the entire universe is filled not with space but with field consciousness. This field of universal consciousness consists of multiple standing waves that penetrate fully the entire universe as it emanates from an underlying unified realm beyond spacetime. Nodes, or manifestations, of standing waves become particles of matter. When not manifested as matter, the field of universal consciousness remains in wave-like form (just as waves upon the 'cosmic ocean'). This wave-form of universal consciousness – the 'unseen' part of the universe - is what some physicists have referred to as being the zero-point field, from which matter (the 5%) manifests.

The fact that, according to quantum theory, the wavefunction of a system collapses under observation indicates that there is an interaction between consciousness and matter. There is now growing belief that consciousness and matter are two complementary aspects of one reality.[5] Out of the underlying field of unified cosmic consciousness emerges the material universe which then defines the boundaries of a physical space-time. All matter-reality is viewed as an emergent product from a unified source field that exists beyond spacetime. Thus, as energy (and then, matter) emerges forth, it becomes embedded within *space* and *time* as science measures it. As such, every living element – both animate and inanimate – is intricately interwoven within the cosmic tapestry. As it is said in The Gospel of Thomas – 'The kingdom is inside you and it is outside of you.'

For the appearance of life, the material universe had to emerge according to coherent and orderly parameters of organization, as we have seen is the case. In a reciprocal fashion, human life itself acts in the form of conscious observers. The act of observation results in the collapse and localization of the field of consciousness. This localization of the consciousness-energy field leads to the appearance of matter, out of which humanity is one of the highest evolved forms. It is an intricate dance of form and formless. In the words of one physicist, 'The Universe is like a corporeal body placed temporarily within the incorporeal Macrocosm.'[6]

The unified source field must therefore act as an information field as it transmits coherent organized information into material manifestation. Scientist-philosopher Ervin Laszlo, in a series of

· · · · · · · · · · · · ·
5   Laszlo, Ervin, 2020. *Reconnecting to The Source*. New York: St. Martin's Press.
6   Jamroz, Wes. 2019. *A Journey through Cosmic Consciousness*. Montreal (QC), Canada. Troubadour Publications, p54

books, has postulated how the underlying cosmic field – which he refers to as the *Akashic Field* – is 'informed' through information. That is, the 'Akashic field' also manifests as a universal information field in nature. Information, says Laszlo, is not only what conscious humans produce, but something that exists independently of humans. It is what he calls the 'ultimate stuff' of all existence. Similarly, Apollo XIII astronaut Edgar Mitchell also stated that information is part of the basic substance of the universe. Mitchell viewed the quantum field as being a holographic field of information. It now appears necessary that mainstream science recognizes that outer space, as they call it, is not empty – nothing is!

It is accepted knowledge, for example, that interactions between things in the physical world operate through a transference of energy; such as gravitational, electromagnetic, nuclear, etc. Energy conveys an effect from one thing to another, from one place to another place. Yet energy itself does not, and cannot, operate within a vacuum. It too requires a medium within which to operate. That is, energy must be conveyed by *something*. Modern science is now beginning to recognize that this intermediary consists of a field and is not an 'empty domain' once referred to as a vacuum. Hence, space is not empty if it is 'filled' with an interacting 'field.'

Likewise, the maverick inventor-genius Nicola Tesla spoke of an 'original medium' that fills space and compared it to what was known at the time in scientific circles as ether. In one of his then unpublished papers – 'Man's Greatest

Achievement' (1907) - he wrote that this original medium becomes matter when a form of cosmic energy (prana) acts on it. And when this 'cosmic action' ceases, matter is once again dissolved into the underlying etheric (akasha) unified field. What may be less well-known is that Tesla was a friend of his contemporary, the spiritual master Swami Vivekananda. According to Vivekananda, the whole universe is composed of two materials: one of which is visible matter; the other, the non-visible, subtle ether (or Akasha). This etheric/ prana/Akasha is an underlying, all-penetrating source dimension out of which the known cosmos is formed, or manifests. Everything that has form, said Vivekananda, evolves out of this ether-field. This prime non-material energizing field gives rise to all the elements of earth, water, air, and fire (the Vedic four elements). That is, all materiality, including atoms, stars, galaxies, the human body – all known creation – emerges from this all-pervasive unified field (ether/prana/Akasha). All came from this unified Source; and at the end of each cycle, all manifested things shall once again return (dissolve) back into this creative and conscious unified energy field. This perspective confirms the knowledge and understanding taught by many of the ancient wisdom traditions. For millennia, various wisdom teachings posited that there is a perceivable field or medium that connects things. This understanding has been proclaimed by mystics and visionaries from the ancient Rishis to modern thinkers such as Sri Aurobindo. It has taken modern, largely western, science a long time to arrive at the 'field medium' realization.

In the late nineteenth century, physicists postulated that space is not empty and passive but filled with an 'invisible subtle energy' which at the time they named the 'luminiferous ether'.[7] They hypothesized that the luminiferous ether produces friction when bodies move through it and thus slows their motion. However, the famous Michelson and Morley experiments at the turn of the twentieth century failed to observe the expected effect, and the subtle or 'luminiferous ether' idea was erased from mainstream science. Later, Einstein's theory of relativity replaced the 'invisible subtle energy' hypothesis with a four-dimensional space-time continuum. Finally, modern physics arrived at the discovery of the 'field effect' that underlies relations among things in the universe and termed this the quantum vacuum. Yet, as we have already discussed, there is no empty space in the universe – there is no 'vacuum.' With the advance toward science's Holy Grail – a 'grand unified theory' (GUT) - in the second half of the twentieth century, the quantum vacuum shifted to describe a 'sea of energy' that reflects the field energy. Some major contemporary physicists still cling to the view that various forms of field effects are manifestations of a 'unified vacuum field.' Again, a denial that this unified field is not only beyond spacetime but also is a unified field of intelligence-information.

The difficulty is that it is neither easy nor clear to show 'evidence' that an underlying intelligence-information field exists as it can only be perceived, by science, through indirect signs. That is, only

. . . .
7   Milutis, Joe. 2006. *Ether: The Nothing That Connects Everything*. Minnesota: University of Minnesota Press

the effects can be perceived – not the source. Yet science has now verified that events, and things, affect each other not only within the known bounds of space and time but also beyond temporal and spatial constraints. The only way for this to occur is through all manifested things – all matter-reality - being connected by a pervasive medium. That is, a unified energetic field. It is not my endeavour here to try to *prove* this to the reader. I am not 'certified' as a physical scientist. Rather, it is my aim to explain and put forth this idea, with a modicum of scientific support, to show that this is a credible possibility. This will then help to orientate the reader for what is to come later in this book – namely, contact with this unified intelligence-information field.

As I have indicated thus far, a unified intelligence-information field that underlays the material universe accounts for the kind of coherent interconnectivity that science has discovered exists. This 'cosmic coherence' appears within this universe at all scales of size and complexity, from the micro-domain of quanta, through all levels of life, to the macro-domain of the cosmos. It can be positively surmised that our known reality has emerged from a fundamental and formless energetic medium of intelligence-information and to which one day all will return. Furthermore, this understanding corresponds to the time-honoured insights of the greatest wisdom traditions. Whilst this phenomenon is very real, it cannot be perceived directly through scientific instruments. It can, however, be *received* through human consciousness, as I discuss in the next chapter.

Chapter Three

Re-Connecting with Cosmic Consciousness

'Humanity has just entered what is probably the greatest transformation it has ever known ... Something is happening in the structure of human consciousness. It is another species of life that is just beginning.'

Pierre Teilhard de Chardin

Philosophers, artists, and scientists have been debating for centuries the questions concerning human consciousness: what it is and how it emerges. The question of human consciousness has also been at the heart of many mystical teachings, although these have tended to be based on revelation rather than investigation and shared research. Over the course of these varied discussions, debates have been divided between the materialistic approach and what may be rather loosely termed as 'spiritual-metaphysical' worldviews. In recent decades, thanks largely to the advance in technologies, scientists have been able to map and study the human brain - including neuronal patterns, brain disorders, and pathways of human thinking. Yet this has led, in main, to an increased certitude among many scientists of a material view of human consciousness. In other words, consciousness exists as a by-product of the physical brain and, as such, cannot exist without brain function. This is the dominant view amongst materialist thinkers and scientists. In more recent years however, and with the further research into nonlocal and holographic phenomena, investigators have been re-visiting mainstream theories of human consciousness. Specifically, as the unified field theory gains more support pointing to the nature of a nonlocal cosmos, a different light is now being shone upon how consciousness may *actually* exist and operate. This subject is the focus of this chapter, as we go further down the conscious rabbit hole.

By recognizing that a consciousness field underlies all material existence, it is easier to accept the notion that human evolution is largely also a question of the evolution of consciousness. Or, to put it another way, humanity's path is one of conscious evolution. And the implication of conscious evolution is that it provides purpose and meaning. To begin, I will examine briefly some of the perspectives and concepts around human consciousness.

Concepts of Consciousness: 1 – The Turbine Theory

As stated, the dominant narrative concerning human consciousness is that it is generated by the brain as a form of by-product. This has been referred to as the 'turbine theory,' whereby just how electricity would be generated by a working turbine as a by-product, so too is human consciousness the by-product of a functioning human brain (motor). This theory postulates human consciousness as being local and produced *from* something tangible. Also, when this producer/motor stops functioning – i.e., the brain ceases to be alive – then consciousness, and related streams of experience, likewise stop. Medical science has gone a long way to validate the 'turbine theory' of consciousness by repeated experiments on how impaired brain functioning results in distorted consciousness.

The basic premise of this understanding of consciousness is that neuronal networks in the human brain have evolved to such a height of complexity that they produce a level of self-consciousness above that of any other animal on the planet (except perhaps dolphins and porpoises). This 'turbine theory' is thus not limited solely to human beings but is applicable to the vast range of living beings on the planet (at least to a level preceding self-reflexive conscious awareness). Here, the degree of consciousness produced by each specific living creature is related to the level of biological complexity.

In recent years there have been renewed calls for a neurological basis for consciousness. For example, neuroscientist Christof Koch (chief scientist at the Allen Institute for Brain Science) has publicly stated that 'consciousness arises within any sufficiently complex, information-processing system. All animals, from humans on down to earthworms, are conscious... That's just the way the universe works.'[8] For Koch, consciousness is a by-product of complexity; thus, complex systems produce varying levels of consciousness, and 'how much consciousness they have depends on how many connections they have and how they're wired up.'[9] Another so-called 'cutting-edge' theory from science is "orchestrated objective reduction" ('Orch OR'), which was first put forward in the mid-1990s by eminent mathematical physicist Sir Roger Penrose, and prominent anesthesiologist Stuart Hameroff.[10] This theory claims that consciousness derives from deeper level, finer scale activities inside brain neurons. Although controversial at the time it has now gained greater credibility as the recent discovery of quantum vibrations in microtubules inside brain neurons appears to corroborate this theory. Yet despite such recent examples of radical new scientific theories of consciousness, they still cling to the basis of an old paradigm 'turbine theory.' In other words, that consciousness is a secondary phenomenon resulting from primary activity located in the human brain. Despite the attempts by mainstream science to strengthen their outlook on consciousness, this 'complexity-produces-consciousness as a by-product' perspective has so many holes. The many holes in this dominant yet conservative theory is owing to a range of experiences that throw doubt upon its validity. Challenges to the turbine theory of consciousness have come, as one example, from

. . . .

8   See http://www.wired.com/2013/11/christof-koch-panpsychism-con-sciousness/all/
9   See http://www.wired.com/2013/11/christof-koch-panpsychism-con-sciousness/all/

10   See http://www.sciencedaily.com/releases/2014/01/140116085105.htm

increasing evidence of 'after death' conscious experiences.

Concepts of Consciousness: 2 – The Cloud Theory

According to the orthodox view, consciousness ceases when the brain dies – i.e., no generator, no current. For many, this may seem like an obvious deduction. However, evidence to the contrary clearly contradicts this theory. Many cases have shown that human consciousness is maintained even though a person is technically declared brain dead. The near-death experience (known as NDE) has been reported by sufficiently large numbers of people who were declared brain-dead. Conscious experience in brain dead people has been reported in almost 25 percent of tracked cases. The NDE phenomenon has now been widely researched and discussed by many credible sources.[11] Furthermore, this phenomenon is not new and there are accounts of NDEs occurring in medieval times.[12] The existence of consciousness – a by-product of brain activity – in the absence of brain function cannot be accounted for by the mainstream turbine theory. There are also numerous indications that human

· · · · · · · · · · · · ·

11 Notable examples include: Alexander, Eben (2012) *Proof of Heaven: A Neurosurgeon's Journey into the Afterlife*. Oxford: Piatkus; Carter, Chris (2010) *Science and the Near-Death Experience; How Consciousness Survives Death*. Rochester: Inner Traditions; Grey, Margot (1986) *Return from Death: An Exploration of the Near-death Experience*. London: Arkana; Laszlo, Ervin; Peake, Anthony (2014) *Immortal Mind: Science and the Continuity of Consciousness Beyond the Brain*. Rochester: Inner Traditions; Lorimer, David (1990) *Whole in One: The near-death experience and the ethic of interconnectedness*. London: Arkana; Moorjani, Anita (2012) *Dying to Be Me: My Journey from Cancer, to Near Death, to True Healing*. New York: Hay House

12 Zaleski, Carol G. (1988) *Otherworld Journeys: Accounts of Near-Death Experience in Medieval and Modern Times*. Oxford: Oxford University Press

consciousness exists in cases of permanent death. That is, many years after a person has died their consciousness remains available for contact and communication, such as through channelling or forms of ESP. However, in these cases the actual person is unable to return to life to corroborate the experience personally. Yet there is now enough credible evidence to put doubt into the mainstream theory that consciousness is solely a by-product of localized brain activity.

The next step, in order to account for these anomalies, might be to suggest that consciousness is in some way conserved beyond the brain - that is, as a nonlocal phenomenon. In this hypothesis, consciousness is something *stored* external to the brain. This can be framed in terms of a 'cloud theory' of consciousness, as this is similar to how information would be conserved on digital platforms accessed by computer networks or other cloud-enabled devices. Likewise, using this analogy, the mainstream 'turbine theory' of consciousness would be akin to an old-fashioned computer without Internet or built-in-memory that would lose all its data once switched off. In this regard, the cloud theory posits consciousness as nonlocal, rather than localized within the brain. Further, the cloud theory allows for not only individual consciousness to be stored, and be recalled, but multiple. This perspective of accessing multiple consciousnesses, beyond our individual one, is reminiscent of Jung's collective unconscious. This theory would appear to support the observations of psychiatrists and consciousness researchers who have induced altered states of consciousness in their clients. When in altered states a vast majority of people have the capacity to recall almost everything that has happened to them. Moreover, their recall is not limited solely to their own experience but can also include the experiences of other people as well.[13] This cloud theory therefore suggests something akin to a collective field of consciousness that makes complete information available relative to the mode of access. This perspective shares similarities with the scientific research on the Akashic Field[14] and Morphic Resonance[15]. However, despite the appropriateness of the cloud theory of consciousness, it too does not account for all observations.

Concepts of Consciousness: 3 – The Hologram Theory

In various recorded accounts of altered state consciousness, it appears that contact/access is not only made with traces of one's nonlocal consciousness but also with distinctive separate conscious intelligence. That is, with an active consciousness that is not the consciousness of a human being. Such experiences, once the realm of shamanic or indigenous traditions, has increasingly entered mainstream culture. Previously, such 'encounters' were labelled as *mystical* or simply conveniently ignored as a quirky anomaly. However, as western

• • • • • • • • • • • •
13   For example, see the work of Stanislav Grof - http://www.stanislavgrof.com/

14   Laszlo, Ervin (2004) *Science and the Akashic Field: An Integral Theory of Everything*. Rochester: Inner Traditions

15   Sheldrake, Rupert (2009) *Morphic Resonance: The Nature of Formative Causation*. Rochester: Park Street Press

science has developed its exploration of the inner realms (such as in transpersonal psychology and similar practices), such experiences have become more widespread and thus need to be accounted for. From this evidence a remarkable conclusion arises: that human consciousness can connect, and often communicate, with conscious entities that not only manifest a sense of self, but also carry distinct memories and information. This experience can neither be accounted for in the mainstream turbine theory nor the more radical cloud theory of consciousness. We now need to consider yet another concept – that consciousness is a cosmic phenomenon with holographic qualities. This is what we may call the 'hologram theory.'

The hologram theory posits that consciousness may manifest *in* spacetime yet originates from a source that exists in a realm beyond spacetime. In other words, consciousness has its origins in a deeper dimension (in a 'unified source field') and yet is manifested as a holographic projection within our quantifiable reality. This concept would suggest that all forms of localized consciousness are manifestations of a unified consciousness field that is beyond spacetime. The implications of this understanding are that consciousness is not 'in' the brain, 'produced' by the brain, nor 'stored' beyond the brain. Rather, it is a localized aspect of a conscious intelligence that infuses the cosmos from its source *beyond* spacetime. This may be a hard pill to swallow for many people. However, when we examine the phenomenon that is consciousness, this perspective actually makes a lot of sense.

The hologram theory goes beyond the incumbent linear thinking which states that consciousness is created as a by-product of the brain. The radical perspective of this new model says that the brain *receives* and *interprets* consciousness, which is infused in the cosmos - but does not *produce* it. This understanding, which is increasingly supported by the very latest scientific findings, points toward a Unified Source Field (USF) as generating what we perceive as spacetime. The materiality of spacetime is thus a holographic projection, coded from an underlying cosmic intelligence-field, which is the source of all conscious intelligence. All things that emerge into physical reality are holographic projections from a deeper dimension of consciousness.

A Deeper Dimension of Reality Consciousness

The understanding that consciousness originates from a deeper dimension of reality has been embraced by many well-known spiritual figures, mystics and visionaries, artists, and even a handful of intuitive scientists. Now it is emerging as the new scientific paradigm for our era. As we have seen, the universe exhibits an incredible – almost impossible – degree of coherence. Now we may know why this is. It is because there is no random cosmos, no separation of materiality and immateriality, no empty space, no 'out there' and 'in here.' Everything – absolutely everything – is an integral part of a nonlocal conscious field whose source is a Unified Source Field (USF) existing beyond the spacetime dimension. Both incredible and yet wonderful.

There is an inherent form of order to the material dimension. The universe, and everything within it, adheres to an evolutionary impulse toward coherence and connection. Perception too, as an attribute of consciousness, trends toward greater conscious coherence (awareness) and connection. At the core of this drive for connectivity, I propose, is an urge for conscious awareness of Source (the Unified Source Field). It is this principal urge (inner drive) that has led to the communications which form Part Two of this book. And as these communications state, it is basically an ongoing communication between ourselves – for we are all aspects of Source.

These understandings give assurance that life is not meaningless nor without purpose. It demonstrates also that there is a source-consciousness – a *Cosmic Mind at Large* – that infuses all known reality. Our connections transcend localized space and time. The human being is inherently connected with the cosmic consciousness. These correlations run throughout our lives, not only within the larger physical universe but also within our very own biological body. Remember – As Above, So Below. It is to an exploration of these quantum resonances that I now turn.

Chapter Four
Quantum Field Resonance

*'The moment it begins to appear that we are deeply connected to the entire universe, science returns...
in a roundabout way, to man and offers him his lost integrity. It does so by anchoring him once more in the cosmos.'*

Vaclav Havel – 'The New Measure of Man'

In the previous chapter I showed that the human being is inherently connected as part of the cosmic consciousness that is emanated from the Unified Source-Field (USF). Through this, the human being has connections that transcend localized space and time. Yet this connectivity not only exists externally but also throughout the staggering amount of chemical and physical reactions that take place within the living organism; notably, the human being. As I discuss in this chapter, communication between cells in the biological organism operate instantaneously through a form of quantum correlation, or quantum resonance. This resonance between cells creates a coherent field throughout the body. This bio-field complements the biochemical flow of information in the organism together with a multidimensional instantaneous-like information field. This, it is now understood, is necessary to ensure the coordinated functioning of the whole organism. Together with biological quantum resonance this starts to present a 'field view' of reality where nothing is separate and where there exist fields within fields. This fits in with what was previously stated about consciousness emanating as a collective field phenomenon from the Unified Source Field.

Research studies from biophysics reveals that quantum coherence operates within living biological systems through biological excitations and biophoton emission. This means that metabolic energy is stored as a form of electromechanical and electromagnetic excitations. It is these coherent excitations that are considered responsible for generating and maintaining long-range order via the transformation of energy and very weak electromagnetic signals. After nearly twenty years of experimental research, Fritz-Albert Popp put forward the hypothesis that biophotons are emitted from a coherent electrodynamic field within the living system.[16] What this describes is that each living cell is giving off, or resonating, a biophoton field of coherent energy. If each cell is emitting this field then the whole living system is, in effect, a resonating field – a ubiquitous nonlocal field. And since it is by the means of biophotons that the living system communicates, then there is near

. . . .

16   Popp, F-A, Li, K H, Mei, W P, Galle, M & Neurohr, R, 'Physical Aspects of Biophotons', *Experientia*, 1988, 44, 576–85

instantaneous intercommunication throughout. This, claims Popp, is the basis for coherent biological organization – referred to as quantum coherence. This implies that all biological organisms continuously emit radiations of light that form a field of coherence and communication. Coherence, it appears, is the byword for living systems.

This discovery led Popp to state that the capacity for evolution rests not on aggressive struggle and rivalry but on the capacity for communication and cooperation. This infers that the in-built capacity for species evolution is not based on the individual alone but rather living systems that are interlinked within a coherent whole.

The biophoton field of the human - the human biofield - is said to consist of numerous partial fields that superpose in multiple ways, and that the overall state of the biofield is constituted by their various interactions. It has also been postulated that the biophoton field forms the basis of memory and regulates biochemical and morphogenetic processes.[17] These latest findings in biophysics have also discovered that all biological organisms are constituted by a liquid crystalline medium; and that DNA is a liquid crystal lattice-type structure, which some refer to as a liquid crystal gel. Further, that body cells are involved in a *holographic* instantaneous communication via the biophoton field resulting in living organisms being permeated by quantum wave forms. As biophysicist Mae-Wan Ho puts it:

· · · · · · · · · · · ·
17   Bischof, M, 'Synchronization and Coherence as an Organizing Principle in the Organism, Social Interaction, and Consciousness', 2008, *NeuroQuantology*, 6, 440–51

... the visible body just happens to be where the wave function of the organism is most dense. Invisible quantum waves are spreading out from each of us and permeating into all other organisms. At the same time, each of us has the waves of every other organism entangled within our own make-up ....[18]

This new information positions each living being within a nonlocal quantum field consisting of wave interferences. The liquid crystalline structure within living systems is also responsible for the direct current (DC) electrodynamic field that permeates the entire body of all animals. It has also been discovered that the DC field has a mode of semi-conduction that is much faster than the nervous system.[19]

Human consciousness, therefore, is not only in a 'wave-interference' relationship with other mind-fields, but also is constantly transmitting and receiving information. Our bodies, as well as our brains, appear to function like receivers/de-coders within an information energy field that is constantly in flux. This suggests that the body forms an extended mind, or informational neural field, with the brain as the receiver and interpreter of the signals. Also, given that DNA is a liquid crystal lattice-type structure which emits biophotons that form a quantum field, we may begin to refer to DNA as being 'quantum DNA.' That is, DNA not only operates in a linear fashion to encode genetic

• • • • • • • • • • • •

18   Ho, M-W, *The Rainbow and the Worm: The Physics of Organisms*, 1998, World Scientific, p116
19   Becker, R O, *The Body Electric*, 1998, William Morrow

information and protein building, but also that it emits a nonlocal energy field. It is within this field that instantaneous communication can occur through a coherent pattern of waves at the quantum level. This suggests that the 97 per cent of human DNA that is not involved in protein building is active within a quantum state. It may well be that increased manifestations of field-like, nonlocal, forms of intuition and knowing (what some have termed speculatively as quantum consciousness) is a property of the portion of DNA that so far has baffled scientists with its function. Within the scope of this book, I am suggesting that the biological organism creates and emits quantum fields that entangle with the greater universal intelligence field. That human beings have an activated self-reflexive conscious awareness shows an ability to knowingly participate within the universal field. And thus, for some people, this can be extended to encompass the Unified Source Field from which the universal field manifests.

Biophysicists are currently discussing whether quantum processes may not be a common denominator for all living processes. As such, a quantum informational field throughout the human body will determine the coherence of our biofields. This raises the question as to what degree human consciousness would be affected by various external impacts, especially in relation to fluctuations in the electromagnetic frequencies caused from terrestrial, solar and cosmic sources. Also, scientific validation of the existence of nonlocal fields of consciousness would at the same time recognize a collective or group consciousness within humanity. This aspect now known as the collective consciousness was well-documented by psychologist Carl Jung. And if the human body functions as a resonating quantum field then it too could be a receiver and transceiver of consciousness beyond the brain. That is, the human body is entangled and in communication with the universal consciousness field, not just the brain.

The Living Intelligence of the Body

From what has been said thus far, it can be hypothesized that DNA exists as a living intelligence, and that the brain works only as a machine-like decoder. The idea of DNA being a living intelligence is not new to many indigenous wisdom traditions. As anthropologist Jeremy Narby has pointed out, shamans who undergo trance states often seem to be communicating with DNA as a means of acquiring knowledge about plants, healing and spirit worlds.[20] Narby explored how Nature is imbued with this form of living intelligence which acts as survival patterns to enable evolutionary growth. Shamans, intuitives, and others who can tap into this living intelligence, find a quantum field that acts as a form of 'design' or blueprint that guides development and evolutionary growth within all living systems. It can be hypothesized that conscious evolution within humanity occurs as more and more people connect with and access the progressing oscillations of the collective field. As philosopher Ervin Laszlo says:

. . . .
20   Narby, J, *Cosmic Serpent: DNA and the Origins of Knowledge*, 1999, Phoenix

The consciousness of individuals can transform instantly, through a sudden insight or revelatory experience, but the consciousness of the species is likely to take time to spread in society. There are people today who live with a traditional or a medieval consciousness, and a few with the consciousness of Stone Age tribes. In the same way there will be humans in the next generation who will achieve transpersonal consciousness, while others, the great majority at first, will persist in the ego-bound consciousness that characterized most of the 20th century. In time, however, a more evolved consciousness is likely to spread over all the continents. It will spread by a form of contagion. An evolved mind is 'infectious', it affects less evolved minds ... A more evolved consciousness will motivate people to develop their own consciousness, it will transform humanity's collective unconscious...most of our species will eventually graduate to transpersonal consciousness, and the next step in the evolution of human consciousness will be achieved.[21]

If it is recognized that the living organism – the body-mind complex – is an entanglement of living intelligence fields, then each person is receiving and decoding nonlocal data. This input of nonlocal data is then processed and the rational-cognitive part of the human brain processes this into linear information that is utilized for social ordering. The direct-intuitive mode of the human brain, on the other hand, correlates this data into abstract-nonlinear information. These two modes of the cognitive and the intuitive are operating simultaneously and represent what we know to be

• • • • • • • • • • • •

21   Cited in Pfeiffer, T & Mack, J (eds), *Mind Before Matter: Visions of a New Science of Consciousness*, 2007, O Books, pp78–9

the respective objective and subjective modes of knowledge.

It can be seen, in this light, that modern societies have largely prioritized the objective interpretation and dismissed the subjective as the imaginative realm. This 'imaginative' realm of subjective experience is most active when we are children, although quickly diminishes as social institutions and peer conditioning intervene to install a consensus social reality. Yet the direct-intuitive mode of perception is an evolutionary trait that is still with us; and, I suggest, is once again coming to the fore. As Part 2 of this book will show, greater forms of communication, such as with the Unified Source Field, are accessed through this direct-intuitive mode.

It is possible that increased sensitivity and receptivity to nonlocal connections, and hence communications, will become more developed in the years ahead. The direct-intuitive mode is a more effective means of comprehension and understanding as it bypasses the cognitive processing that act as filters. Also, the direct-intuitive mode operates outside of linguistic barriers, which may explain why many altered state experiences have offered similar results. Many traditional rituals and wisdom traditions function to break down the dominant consensus cognition. In fact, the use of specific sounds/rhythms (drumming, chanting), fasting, frenzied dancing, etc., may work to stress the cognitive and rational mode of perception to the point that, unable to cope or 'control' the situation, an alternate state of consciousness comes to the fore. Shamans are able to enter the nonlocal state and, by mastering nonlocal connections, interpret the information they absorb and bring it back to the local rational world. What was once considered to be the realm of the supernatural can now be seen as accessing the universal field. Shamans, and similar practitioners, were those people who first learnt how to utilize human capacity for accessing the universal consciousness field, and to bring this knowledge back to a localized physical reality.

The nonlocal field perception of reality is now being experienced by more and more people, from all walks of life, who are accessing an altered state of consciousness, whether it be from a prescribed ritual, religious/spiritual exercises, or from spontaneous bursts of intuition and insight. Some of these experiences have been categorized as 'extraordinary encounters,' and have been noted to affect a person's inner state as well as their physiology.

Psychologists Kenneth Ring and Margot Grey had both conducted studies on people who reported near-death experiences. It was found that they often returned from the experience with a changed worldview, one that recognized a living, intelligent cosmos and the primacy of consciousness. Ring's study groups almost all tended to agree that their experiences reflected a purposive intelligence and that they were part of an accelerating evolutionary current that is driving humanity toward higher consciousness. Both Ring and Grey concluded that such encounters into the nonlocal realm appeared to offer a gateway to a 'radical, biologically based transformation of the human personality'.[22]

Ring and Grey believe that having an extraordinary experience with a nonlocal connectedness actually impacted the human nervous system, possibly releasing transformative energy, or at least in some form affecting the biological system of the individual. They view people who have experienced the nonlocal realm, whether through the near-death experience or other methods, as being the forerunners of a new species of humanity. Both agree that the real significance of such nonlocal encounters may lie in their 'evolutionary implications for humanity.' Ring, who has studied the near-death experience for nearly 40 years, has concluded that encounters with a nonlocal reality appear to accelerate a *psychophysical* transformation, and that such encounters may well herald what he calls the *shamanizing of modern humanity*. Such experiences, he notes, help to develop humanity's latent capacities for a direct, intuitive mode of perception. By embracing the 'field-view' of reality as part of a unified intelligence, this may help to stimulate an intuitive mode of perception that, in turn, values connection, communication and compassion over older values.[23]

What I feel all this is demonstrating is that not only the human brain, but the whole body, functions in resonance with the whole cosmos – as fields within fields. Humans are localized energy

• • • • • • • • • • • • •
22   Ring, K, *The Omega Project: Near-Death Experiences, UFO Encounters, and Mind at Large*, 1992, William Morrow, p168
23   See my book *The Phoenix Generation: A New Era of Connection, Compassion & Consciousness* (2014)

fields in resonance with ever greater fields that are all part of one immense, unified sea of conscious intelligence. This is the missing link between objective science and subjective experience. As psychiatrist Ede Frecska puts it: 'Nonlocality is to the physicist what interconnectedness is to the mystic; the quantum hologram is the foundation through which to understand virtually all paranormal phenomena.'[24] What this suggests too is that when the human brain interacts with local aspects of the universe through a cognitive-linear perception, it forms what we know as the consensus view of reality. Yet when our body-brains, for whatever reasons, suddenly (or gradually) enter into a direct-intuitive interaction with the universal field, then we have a unique perception of non-ordinary states of consciousness.

These forays into direct-intuitive and nonlocal consciousness used to be the domain of experienced practitioners (shamans, mystics, psychics) who may have undergone rigorous and lengthy training. Our 'everyday consciousness' of the local view of the universe is largely unprepared for the realms of non-ordinary reality. In the present era, and in western civilization especially, the nonlocal mode of perception (commonly referred to as subjective experience) has not been encouraged, or at times not even recognized. Because of this, it has atrophied and become the province of the mystical or esoteric realms. It may be that the local cognitive view of reality has gained dominance

· · · · · · · · · · · ·
24   Strassman, R, Wojtowicz, S, Eduardo Luna, L, Frecska, E, *Inner Paths to Outer Space: Journeys to Alien Worlds through Psychedelics and Other Spiritual Technologies*, 2008, Park Street Press, p196

for it allows an increased sense of individualism, favoured by the ego, and as such is the sphere of power, money, competition and greed. The nonlocal, quantum field resonance view of reality, however, embraces cooperation, connection, correspondence and collective comprehension. This form of consciousness is very likely to be an evolutionary development that has been gradually emerging within humankind over some time. As Dr Richard Bucke stated in his popular work *Cosmic Consciousness,*

> The simple truth is, that there has lived on the earth, 'appearing at intervals', for thousands of years among ordinary men, the first faint beginnings of another race ... This new race is in the act of being born from us, and in the near future it will occupy and possess the earth.[25]

Overall, social-cultural-material forces are slow to react to the need for an evolving paradigm of human consciousness. Throughout recorded history many individuals have experienced, intuited, or been gifted, an awareness of the greater cosmic unified intelligence, as shall be explored further in Chapter Six. There has always been a stirring of the evolutionary impulse within humanity, manifesting also through events and actions upon the physical world. According to Gopi Krishna,

> I can safely assert that the progress made by mankind in any direction, from the

· · · · · · · · · · · ·
25   Bucke, R, *Cosmic Consciousness: A Study in the Evolution of the Human Mind*, 1972/1901, The Olympia Press

subhuman level to the present, has been far less due to man's own efforts than to the activity of the evolutionary forces at work within him. Every incentive to invention, discovery, aesthetics, and the development of improved social and political organizations invariably comes from within, from the depths of his consciousness by the grace of … the superintelligent Evolutionary Force in human beings.[26]

This 'superintelligent Evolutionary Force' that Krishna speaks of could very well be the Unified Source Field from which all physical reality manifests. This force runs through everything because *everything* is a part of it. As consciousness explorer Chris Bache puts it – 'the purpose of spiritual awakening appears to be not escaping from physical existence…but awakening ever more completely *inside* physical existence and participating in its continuing self-emergence through our awakening.'[27]

Part of this awakening is to recognize that human consciousness is a tangible force for real and actionable change. New science, alongside explorations from brave consciousness researchers, are providing a long-overdue revival of such cosmic comprehension. Research alone from the frontiers of quantum physics and quantum biology suggests that there are valid experiences that reach our consciousness without having passed through

• • • • • • • • • • • •

26   Krishna, G, *Higher Consciousness and Kundalini*, 1993, F.I.N.D. Research Trust, p166

27   Bache, Christopher M. 2019. *LSD & The Mind of the Universe*. Rochester, VT: Park Street Press, p36

our senses. It is no longer enough just to base our understanding upon the rational and the logical. It is time to admit that reality is more than just a 'solid object' perspective. We are enmeshed within an animated, energetic and conscious unified field of life.

With this understanding we come to appreciate that the physical reality that humans inhabit belongs to a vaster cosmic living intelligence that is, to use a familiar word, *soulful*. What else can be said other than, it is high time to *re-soul* our worldview.

Chapter Five
Re-Souling our Worldview

'When we understand that the longing originates in the soul, new ways of imagining the world have to be sought, and these new ways have to be conscious soul ways.'

Robert Sardello

Humanity has spent so much of its time trying to 'solidify' the world. As a species, we've been driving the human mind further and further away from the interior realms and into exterior pursuits. If anything, it has been a path of great distraction. The more serious consequences of this is that it has driven human civilization to its current peak of materiality, corruption, and alienation. In these times, the interior life is but a shallow backdrop to the deep materiality of the external world that draws people *away from* themselves. In contrast, the ancient Egyptians are known to have produced the first maps, circa four thousand years ago - yet they were not maps of the physical world, but of the *otherworld*. They mapped the regions where the soul travelled. Similarly, in the famous 'The Book of the Dead,' the Egyptians mapped the journey of the soul in its transformation beyond the physical world. Over the course of western history, from the ancient to the modern world, there have been fundamental shifts in how humanity has perceived the connection and communion between itself and the larger cosmos.

> In the far distant past people were aware they lived in a Sacred Order where Hidden beings, intermediaries between earth and heaven, still connected the dimension of the physical world to the unseen dimension which ensouled it. There was no rigid line drawn between what was imagination and what was reality, because what was imagined *was* reality. The human soul was part of the greater Soul of the Cosmos...[28]

In the ancient world, the World Soul – or *anima mundi* – was very real. For Plato, the World Soul was the interrelated patterns from which the cosmos unfolded. Yet Plotinus is perhaps the philosopher most closely connected with the notion of the World Soul. Plotinus viewed all reality as essentially spiritual, and the source of the cosmos as unlimited and infinite. The name he most often gave to this unlimited source – when he was forced to use language – was 'the One.' It symbolised the simplicity of unity - that which lies beyond our descriptions, our categories, and our divisions. From 'the One' emanates the *Nous* – the universal principle of Mind. Yet this is not referring to the

· · · · · · · · · · · · ·
28   Baring, Anne (2013) *The Dream of the Cosmos: A Quest for the Soul.* Dorset, Archive Publishing, p80

mind that is manifested within us – the localized mind - but rather it is us, and everything else, that exists within the greater Mind. The idea of 'the One' is also, it seems, the Unified Source Field by another name.

For Plotinus, all patterns of intelligence and order are embedded in the *Nous* - it is what shapes the fabric of perceived reality. The *Nous*, the universal Mind (not the Source Field that is beyond spacetime) emanates out into the World Soul forming a continuity, with no division. In Plotinus's schema, the immaterial World Soul then gives birth to Nature, a reality brought into being and animated by the World Soul, which is itself an emanation from *Nous* – and all belonging within the matrix of 'the One' (Unified Source Field). Overall, it is a harmonious unity of order, pattern, entanglement, and beauty.

The role of philosophy for Plotinus was for it to awaken our true inner vision and to show the world as it truly is, rather than through secondary forms. Plotinus wanted to compel others to break through to a purity of perception and understanding. This is in alignment with the ancient Greek mystery traditions that viewed Nature as alive, dynamic, and permeated by a spirit that was open to transformation. Yet the civilizational drive into present-day modernity has been, like Eliot's 'Wasteland' or the Fisher King's perpetual winter, collectively estranging the human being from the soul of the world. We have lost touch with the essential unity of our existence. It is time now to step upon the way back home. It is a path that for aeons the greatest poets, shamans, and visionaries, as well as artists, musicians and mystics of all cultures, have kept alive in the world. It is the magic that never died.

Magic Never Died

> *God is alive, magic is afoot*
> *God is alive, magic is afoot*
> *God is afoot, magic is alive*
> *Alive is afoot, magic never died*

Leonard Cohen

The worldview I am proposing is not a concept but an experiential understanding of life that goes beyond our individual, limited selves. The time is now ripe to discuss such a subject. Before the rise of the psychological sciences there was no cultural language to explore the subconscious. The inner landscape of the human being was quietly explored and navigated by the mystics, seers, adepts, and initiates that kept their traditions away from the masses – away from persecution. Magic too has always been present in its various guises. Magic, in its original form, is that which concentrates and radiates the mind; it is a deep penetrating force-field of compassion and communion. Magic may shock the profane, yet it has existed as a core experience long before we had any sense of what it actually was. As historian and scholar Arthur Versluis notes,

> The reason that magic is not in good standing in the West is that it is based upon

> the fundamental unity of man and cosmos and so is in conflict with the inherent dualism of the modern outlook. But magic will be in existence long after the modern era has disappeared: it cannot be otherwise, for magic is the physical expression of the eternal, inner, spiritual transmutation. [29]

When it comes to the 'eternal, inner, spiritual transmutation' there are no absolute laws, just the continual unfolding. And as Versluis notes, magic is a perspective that sees, and supports, the fundamental unity of humanity and cosmos. What is being discovered today by the latest science is nothing less than a revival of ancient perspectives of magic. Yet the ancient Egyptians knew this well.

For the ancient Egyptians, magic was not so much seen as a series of human practices or rituals but rather as the essential energy that pervades the cosmos. It was an underlying pervasive energy that humans could access, activate, and potentially direct. The Egyptians understood this magic to be in the form of a god, named Heka, which represented the primal cosmic energy that permeated all levels of existence. It was an energy that animated the bodies of gods and humans, as well as the plants and the stones. This cosmic principle in one's own nature was also the underlying animating energy of the cosmos. In those times there was not the vocabulary that is extant today for observing and describing the cosmos. The Egyptians, for example, expressed themselves through the visual language of hieroglyphics. In this language, the

29   Versluis, Arthur (1986) *The Philosophy of Magic*. London, Arkana, p129

deep animating force of the human soul came from a communion with the spiritualizing force of the cosmos. From their language, translated into our own, we know this as magic. Yet to them it was a different form of magic, and totally unlike that which we understand today. And yet, if we take a glance at the quirky weirdness of the quantum world with its uncertainty principle and quantum entanglement, we are seeing the same form of magic that inspired the Egyptians. As the eminent science-fiction writer Arthur C. Clarke famously stated as one of his laws - *Any sufficiently advanced technology is indistinguishable from magic.* Magic is the mysterious glue that entangles and connects, and it also mirrors the 'magical' quantum collapse into *being*.

Quantum physics shows that through measurement, or rather observation, quantum energy 'collapses' into a particle or wave function. And yet this terminology is misleading - it is a misconception of how we understand sight and observation. We don't *observe* particles or phenomena at a distance – we are already participating in their existence. The observer effect should really be changed to saying the *participatory effect*. As discussed in the previous chapters, consciousness is a participatory field phenomenon. In our known reality, we participate in a conscious, intelligent universal field where, according to the Hermetic saying, the centre is everywhere and the circumference nowhere. This view correlates somewhat with the words of famed theoretical physicist John Archibald Wheeler:

The universe does not exist 'out there' independent of us. We are inescapably bringing about that which appears to be happening. We are not only observers. We are participators. In some strange sense this is a participatory universe.[30]

Another way of re-phrasing the deceptive 'wave collapse' is to refer to it as *coming into being*. What is taking place is a quantum act of creation. The underlying quantum energy field is a cosmic playground of participatory creation.

The quantum realm is the magical realm, where human consciousness mingles with the unified field with the potential to manifest creative imagination into matter-reality. We could call this the Higgs Boson Effect. The Higgs Boson – also somewhat ironically referred to as the 'God Particle' – was first proposed by a team of physicists in 1964 (and not just one guy called Higgs!). Several other physicists from the 1960s onwards also speculated and hypothesized on the Higgs Field effect. This enquiry led to a forty year search within the international physics community and eventually culminated in the construction of the world's most expensive experimental test facility and the largest single machine in the world – the CERN Large Hadron Collider.[31] After many experiments and independently verified research, CERN announced on 14th March 2013 that there

• • • • • • • • • • • •

30   Cited in Skolimowski, H. (1993). *A Sacred Place to Dwell: Living With Reverence Upon the Earth*. Shaftesbury, Dorset, p82.
31   The *Conseil Européen pour la Recherche Nucléaire* (English - The European Organization for Nuclear Research). The Large Hadron Collider is a particle collider that lies in a tunnel 27 kilometres/17 miles in circumference beneath the France-Switzerland border.

were strong indications that the Higgs boson had been found. It was what they had been looking for all along. And finally, after much mental focusing and scientific ritual, with instruments and precise application, a phenomenon materialized into reality. Perhaps it will go down in history as one of the most complex, community-led, conjuring tricks in the annals of science. Or maybe it will just be seen as yet another proof that the scientific method works. Is searching for the Higgs boson – as the quantum excitation of the Higgs field - any different from magical correspondences with non-visible fields of force? Perhaps applied science then is the modern name for the magical pursuit of eternal truths?

Genuine magic can be considered as the science and art of communion with the cosmos and the manifestation of our deepest will into materiality. Magic is the spiritualizing force that animates the human soul, and which communes with the soul of the world, the *anima mundi*. We have also hidden this magic within our sciences, our technologies, and within our human memories and emotions; and yet it is the pervasive force which entangles all things together and from which the immaterial becomes material.

We are finally regaining the understanding through the new sciences that our knowledge is not discovered or given to us but are part of the reality that is being continually created by us. Our engagement with the intelligence of the cosmic mind is part of a grander unfolding where *everything* is evolving – especially our perceptions of the universe and of cosmic reality.

As human beings, we each interact with the world differently because we *perceive* the world differently. In interacting differently, we each contribute to creating a different world. And a civilization's worldview is its most precious possession. The basic, fundamental understanding is that we cannot observe the world without changing it. The worldview we adopt articulates the context for interpreting and understanding the human condition. In each era, we articulate the human condition in the context of our times. And this comprehension comes as a response to a shifting and unfolding understanding of the cosmos and the current concept of reality. Our perspectives on the world and the cosmos have been changing dramatically over recent years. Humanity is gradually metamorphosing out of its cocoon of cosmic quarantine.

As we expand our view of the cosmos, we will become more intelligible to ourselves, and more capable of recognizing the true nature of reality. Until we reach that state, all truths are relative. Christopher Bache, through his own journeys into transpersonal psychology, came to understand that the entire universe is a unified organism of extraordinary design reflecting a massive 'Creative Intelligence.' We shall come to explore more of Bache's experiences with the 'massive Creative Intelligence' in the next chapter. For now, we shall do well to reflect on what the Greek Orphic Mysteries of 2,500 years ago spoke: 'I am a child of earth and starry heaven, but my race is of heaven alone.'

Chapter Six

Communing with the Cosmic Mind

'What is emerging is a consciousness of unprecedented proportions, the entire human family integrated in a unified field of awareness. The species reconnected with its Fundamental Nature. Our thoughts turned to Source Consciousness.'

Chris Bache

I ended the previous chapter with the thought that as we expand our view of the cosmos, not only will we come to understand ourselves better but also the true nature of reality that exists beyond current perceptual limitations. At this time, it can be said that we are perceptual infants. Within the previous chapters in this Part One, I have attempted to give a broad overview of how the latest findings in the quantum sciences and consciousness research can provide a renewed vista upon how the cosmos operates. This view puts forth the role of the human as an observer/participator encoded as a sacred principle within the universal laws. As a human being, we are a participant in the unfolding of cosmic reality. We are a part of it as opposed to being apart from it. Within this perspective, our role is needed in order to 'collapse the wave function' for matter-reality to manifest, or emerge, from its background of energetic potentials. Yet for the universe to emerge within spacetime, perhaps there was needed an 'observer' within the grander macro dimension beyond spacetime. What has been suggested so far within these pages is that the known universe, as a physical construct, has also been *collapsed into emergence* from a Greater Observer beyond the known confines of this spacetime reality. Might this Observer be the grand 'Cosmic Mind' that so many people have referred to since antiquity as the Sacred Creator? Might not this be the intelligence of the Unified Source Field?

As mentioned, the famous Greek philosopher Plato wrote of the realm of Pure Ideas from which trickle down the counterfeit scraps that form this diluted realm of lesser reality. As discussed in Chapter Two, this *pure realm* (i.e., Unified Source Field) was spoken of by Pythagoras as *Kosmos*, and Plotinus as *The One*. It is the realm of no-space, no-time, and no-form that we have no-real words to describe. The view I have put forth is that the known physical universe is in continual correspondence – in real-time - with its energetic origin, or Source. Human correspondence with this 'source realm' has been the remit of mystics, sages, and seers since time immemorial. Within the last century the Indian sage Sri Aurobindo spoke of the Absolute Truth-Consciousness (pure being-consciousness) from which emerged a 'Supermind' that lay between it and the physical universe.

Aurobindo's body of philosophy, generally referred to as integral yoga, consisted of preparing the human being to actualize a merging with the supramental consciousness of the Supermind, transforming both the individual and life upon Earth in the process. Aurobindo's Supermind is the creative intelligence out of which the construct of spacetime materialized. Other mystics and sages have spoken in similar terms of correspondence with a Greater Mind or Creative Intelligence with which one can 'merge' their consciousness. Such knowledge has been in existence, again, from time immemorial, mostly relegated to forms of 'ancient wisdom' or various mystical lineages – and always far from the mainstream narrative.

The Swiss psychologist C.G. Jung can be credited with popularising in the West the notion of expansive fields of consciousness that exist beyond linear, mechanical models. He was perhaps the first to fully realize that what we see playing out upon the global stage is largely a projection, or symptom, of the unconscious psyche of humanity. Jung coined the term 'collective unconscious' in his 1916 essay 'The Structure of the Unconscious' and went on to articulate his ideas further in later publications. He explored how 'primordial images' - or 'archetypes' as he came to call them - belonged to an underlying unconscious psyche and were not individually acquired. He noted how there is a 'psychic stratum' that includes the psychic experiences of human ancestry right back to its earliest beginnings. Importantly, Jung considered that humanity's collective unconscious does not develop individually but is inherited. Or rather, we gain access to a reservoir of stored psychic experience. This has now become integrated into mainstream psychological understanding. Is this so very different from the recognition that the human 'mind' can access even larger reservoirs of experience – such as the Cosmic Mind?

In the remainder of this chapter I would like to explore the ideas and experiences of Chris Bache, professor emeritus in the Department of Philosophy and Religious Studies at Youngstown State University where he taught for 33 years. This professor administered 73 high doses of LSD in controlled settings as part of his private research into transpersonal journeying. His experiences were remarkable and provide a modern-day account of communion with the cosmic mind. What Bache encountered was not the *pure realm* of Plato's unchanging, eternal Ideas, but vast *living* dynamic forces. Bache explains how he came into contact with higher orders of 'intentionality and power' that operate beyond the notion of spacetime. These forces, he says, are those that inform human experience. Beyond our present sense of reality lies a much deeper reality that influences humanity in profound but unknown ways. Human beings are not, he realized, free agents on the world stage. However, at the same time, we are much more than this. Bache came to see humanity as a spectacular single organism with intelligent networks running through it. These interconnected, integrated networks within the organism of humanity did not negate our individual agency but were the operations of a conscious intelligence at a deeper level. From this meta-perspective, Bache was able to see beyond the stories and beliefs that human history has imprinted upon itself.

The 'deeper reality' that Chris Bache experienced was, in his view, the fabric of existence itself. He came to refer to this as the Mind of the Cosmos – a transcendent source from which manifests all known life and matter-reality. In order to know the universe at these levels, Bache declares that one must *become* a citizen of these levels. Or even further – a person must *become* the levels themselves. To accomplish this, the 'smaller sense of self' or personal ego must be given up. Bache puts it more succinctly by saying that giving up everything is simply the price of inheriting everything else. On a more human note, he admits that he doesn't understand how it all works. Once a person moves outside of their perceptive limitations, the 'rules of the game' change. As Bache experienced in his mid-way journey in sessions 22-23:

> *The great difficulty I have is describing the enormity of what is being birthed. The true focus of this creative process is not individuals but all humanity. It is actually trying to awaken our entire species. What is emerging is a consciousness of unprecedented proportions, the entire human family integrated in a unified field of awareness. The species reconnected with its Fundamental Nature. Our thoughts turned to Source Consciousness.*[32]

· · · · · · · · · · · ·
32   Bache, Christopher M. 2019. *LSD & The Mind of the Universe*. Rochester, VT: Park Street Press, p131

What Bache *felt* through this immersion within the Mind of the Cosmos was an impulse for humanity to turn to 'Source Consciousness.' As a collective species we have lost our memory of being integrated in a unified field of awareness. As the reader will soon discover, this is the exact same message that is given in Part Two in the communications from the unified source field. This is why I considered it of importance to explore Bache's personal experiences here.

What we learn from these explorations is that matter is similar to a blank canvas upon which a painter then paints upon. In this respect, the unified field is the painter, and humanity are coloured fragments upon the vast canvas of matter. We act with consciousness and in communion with the Mind at Large. We do not act apart from this grander consciousness but as a part of it. To use another well-known allegory, we are as actors upon a stage, entering into life as an actor dons a new costume from the wardrobe. To quote the famous words of Shakespeare:

All the world's a stage,

and all the men and women merely players;

they have their exits and their entrances,

and one man in his time plays many parts,

As You Like It, Act II, Scene VII

Significantly, Bache came to the realization that some of our thoughts, strictly speaking, are not our own. In session 28 the following was experienced:

> *We usually assume that the thoughts*
> *rising within our individual awareness*
> *are "our" thoughts, our private creation.*
> *Yet now I saw that some of these thoughts*
> *are not "ours" at all in a strict sense, but*
> *the registering in our local awareness of*
> *a collective thought rising in the species-*
> *mind as a whole, a thought that had been*
> *initiated at a deeper, centralized level of*
> *intelligence.*[33]

In other words, collective fields of thought flow through human awareness, both consciously and unconsciously. There are no solid boundaries between these fields, as thoughts ripple across them as across water.

I wish now to present one of two lengthier extracts from Bache as his explorations and experiences are significant in providing a context for Part Two of this book. This first extract is taken from what Bache called his *Cosmic Tour* session:

> *A circle opened around me and created*
> *a space that became an arena of dialogue*
> *between myself and a larger Consciousness.*
> *I discovered much to my surprise that this*
> *field was responsive to my thoughts. When*
> *I first discovered this, I had the ecstatic*

. . . .
33   Ibid., p157

*sensation of confronting an enormous
Intelligence that included and surrounded
my own. "That's right," it communicated
to me. "That's exactly what is happening."*

*I began to ask it questions, and it answered
by orchestrating my experience in the circle.
It was an extremely subtle process, and the
line between "my" consciousness and this
larger Consciousness was often invisible
to me. At times my reaction to an answer
interacted with what I was being shown to
sidetrack the lesson being given. I learned
that I could stop these unwanted deviations
by taking control of my thoughts. I could
"clear the board" by stopping my reactions
and waiting for the space I was in to clear.
Once my mind was still, the lesson would
continue.*

*After some intervening experiences, I was
brought to an encounter with a unified field
underlying all physical existence. I was
confronting an enormous field of blindingly
bright, incredibly powerful energy. This
energy was the single energy that composed
all existence. All things that existed were
but varied aspects of its comprehensive
existence. Experiencing it was extremely
intense and carried with it a sense of
ultimate encounter...*

*... For the next several hours, this
Consciousness took me on an extraordinary
tour of the universe. It was as though It
wanted to show me Its work. It appeared
to be the creator of our physical universe.*

It would take me somewhere or open me to some experience, and I would come to understand some aspect of the workings of the universe. Over and over again, I was overwhelmed at the magnitude, the subtlety, and the intelligence of what I was witnessing.

"That's incredible."

"I'm beginning to understand."

I was repeatedly left breathless by the beauty of the design I was seeing…

… At one point, I was taken through a complex labyrinth of churning forces until I emerged above the turbulence into a wonderfully spacious and calm experiential field. I was told that we had come through the emotions of human experience. They had a restless, gnawing quality to them and composed such a mass of tangled energy that I was not surprised that they could blot out this subtler domain of peace and tranquility…

… Finally, I was lifted into a particularly spacious and peaceful dimension. As I remembered this dimension, I was overcome by an overwhelming sense of homecoming and felt fully the tragedy of having forgotten this dimension for so long. I cannot describe how poignant this was. Being fully restored to this dimension would be worth any cost. I asked what had happened, and It explained that we had left time. Then It said, "We never intended so many to get caught in time." It felt like

time was simply one of the many creative experiments of the multidimensional universe I was being shown.

   Though these experiences were extraordinary in their own right, the most poignant part of today's session was not the dimensions of the universe I was witnessing, but what my seeing them meant to the Creative Consciousness I was with. It seemed so pleased to have someone to show Its work to. I sensed that It had been waiting billions of years for embodied consciousness to evolve to the point where we could at last begin to see, to understand, and to appreciate what had been accomplished in our self-evolving universe. I felt the loneliness of this Intelligence, having created such a masterpiece and having no one to appreciate Its work, and I wept. I wept for its self-isolation and in awe of the profound love that had accepted this isolation as part of a larger plan. Behind creation lies a Love of extraordinary proportions. The Intelligence of the universe's design is matched by the depth of Love that inspired it.[34]

This extract is an incredible description of a form of communication taking place between an individual mind (Chris Bache) and a field of unified intelligence. It also relays a deep emotional connection - *an overwhelming sense of homecoming.*

. . . .
34   Ibid., p112-116

When we come to Part Two and the ABE material, we shall see that ABE gave the title for these series of communications as 'The Way Back Home.' ABE, likewise, frames these messages as a form of re-connecting with a home source.

An apt phrase that Bache encountered in his transpersonal sessions was – '*If only you could see reality as it truly is!*' Indeed, if only we could! So far, we've had to go out of ourselves in order to find ourselves again. And yet, maybe this is all now changing? What if humans could 'tune in' to this unified 'Mind of the Cosmos' from where they are sitting right now? It is my own personal sense that the 'veils of perception' are thinning, and that awareness of expanded consciousness field communication is now occurring. In fact, it's what creative artists have referred to as 'inspiration' for thousands of years. Instead of nominating the source of such inspiration as the *Muses*, why not just cut out the middle person and say directly that inspiration comes from a communion with the Source Field? Are we not, after all, interacting continuously with this unified field of conscious intelligence through our own localized fields of consciousness?

This recognition is deeply humbling. It serves to strip away the layers of our conditioned personality – the ego self. It is, in one way, a process of experiencing the death of the ego. The second lengthier extract from Chris Bache comes from the session he named as *Dying into Oneness* and it covers this theme well:

As I expanded into what I was seeing, I was becoming larger. I learned by becoming what I was knowing. I discovered the Universe not by knowing it from the outside but by tuning to that level of my being where I was that thing. All I can do at this point is to sketch the highlights of the experiences that followed, which will not do justice either to their cognitive structure or to their experiential intensity.

What stood out for me in the early stages was the interconnectedness of everything to form a seamless whole. The entire universe was an undivided, totally unified, organic whole. I saw various breakthroughs – quantum theory, Bell's Theorem, morphogenetic field theory, holographic theory, systems theory, the grand unified theory – as but the early phases of science's discovery of this innate wholeness. I knew that these discoveries would continue to mount until it would become impossible for us not to see the Universe for what it is: a single unified organism of extraordinary complexity and subtlety reflecting a vast Creative Intelligence – the Mind of the Universe. The intelligence and love that was responsible for what I was seeing kept overwhelming me and filling me with reverential awe.

The Unified Field that was underlying my physical existence completely dissolved all boundaries. As I moved deeper into it, all borders fell away; all appearances of division were ultimately illusory. No boundaries between incarnations, between human beings, between species, even between matter and spirit. The world of individuated existence was not collapsing into an amorphous mass, as it might sound, but rather was revealing itself to be an exquisitely diversified manifestation of a single entity.

As my experience of this seamless universe progressed, I came to discover that I was not exploring a universe "out there," as I had in session 19, but a universe that "I" in some essential way already was. These experiences were leading me step by step into a deeper embrace of my own reality. I was exploring the universe as a dimension of my own existence, slowly remembering aspects of my being that I had lost contact with. This exploration seemed to answer a cosmic need not only to know but to be known.

Initially I was on a cosmic tour not unlike session 19 when I realized again that this larger field of consciousness that I was with (or in) had been waiting a long time to be recognized. Again I began to weep as I felt its heartfelt longing to be known. Then I asked something I had not asked before. I asked, "Who am I talking to?" With that question my experiential field began to change, and I dropped into a new level of reality. It was as though I fell into a deeper operational level where I discovered that I was, in fact, with MYSELF. The creative impulse that had been "other" to me at the previous level was at this level myself.

This mysterious progression repeated itself many times and in many variations. It continued for hours. I would be at one level of reality far beyond physical diversity, and as I sought to know this reality more deeply, I would experience a kind of dying, a falling away, and would slip into a new level where I would discover that this duality too was but another facet of Myself. Over and over again, in detailed progressions, I was led to the same fundamental encounter.

No matter how many times I died or how many different forms I was when I died, I kept being caught by this massive SOMETHING, this IT. I could not leave IT, could not escape IT, could not not be IT. No matter how many adventures I had been on, I had never stepped outside IT, never stopped being IT. There simply was no outside to My Being. There was no other in existence.[35]

When we strip away the boundaries, the veils of perception, we come to the grand realization that everything is *MYSELF*. That is – *I am.* Again, this relates with one of the messages from ABE. In chapter nine, the following question is asked – *If our consciousnesses are intertwined, then is it possible*

35   Ibid., p122-24

that you know our questions before we ask them? It is like having a conversation between ourselves? Below is an edited version of ABE's answer:

> One could say that yes, for that is how we would see it. Like the whole universe is mad, talking to oneself...You have become so frightened by it in a way, and in the knowing that it is not really what I am; and 'I am' is a lot more expansive and inclusive. You can realize that life isn't so terrifying, but a great expression of one thing and you can go ahead and just live, just participate. ABE.

Chris Bache came to understand that the transformation of humanity was perhaps the only thing the Cosmic Mind really cared about. Furthermore, that this unified creative intelligence really did care – I mean, *really, deeply care*. It's a beautiful scenario. It is encaptivating. It is also wonderfully enchanting and immersive. We are a part of everything and apart from nothing. This is the way back home – the journey back to ourselves. For our *self* is every self.

Let us turn now to Part Two, where we begin the way back home.

PART TWO

The Way Back Home:
The ABE Communications

Chapter Seven
The ABE Communications - what are they?

'Remember - The harvest of the seed is in preparation of the food.'

ABE

How I came to be involved in these communications was a surprise even to me. It all came quite literally 'out of the blue,' as they say. I will do my best to give a brief yet accurate history of how this relationship came about and how we gathered the subsequent material that forms this central part of the book. I would now like to introduce the reader to Nicola Mortimer, the lady who receives and shares the communications with the Unified Source Field.

The first time I knew of Nicola was when I received an email out of the blue, sometime around late summer 2018. She wrote to say that she had recently read an article of mine and something compelled her to get in touch. We corresponded on this topic and slowly, and courteously, began to discuss similar topics and articles. We then moved onto messaging through social media and began corresponding in a more informal way - more like buddies. It didn't take us long to find out that not only had we been born in the same city in England, but that we had grown up just down the road from each other – literally, just a couple of miles between us. We had, it seemed, a common bond.

It was then that Nicola ventured a step further, and asked me, somewhat timidly, what I thought about life after death, and the idea that a part of us lives on, indefinitely. I say timidly, because Nicola wasn't sure how I would react to this. I reassured her that my mind was not only very open to such concepts, but that I had written a fair amount of material on issues such as collective and universal consciousness, the conscious universe, and multidimensional reality. This seemed to put her more at ease. And it was perhaps also the reason why Nicola ventured another step. There was something else she wished to confide in me and to share. It was about a series of communications she said she had been receiving. Receiving? I asked. How do you mean by 'receiving'? No, these were not communications by email but from a 'contact' or 'source' that Nicola could hear within herself. I was intrigued and asked her to tell me more. She was very shy in this respect and was hesitant to say too much. I suspected she was wary about what I might think of her – whether I might consider her slightly odd. But far from it, Nicola seems to me to be one of the most down-to-Earth people I know. I encouraged her to send some of the material over to me, just to take a glance. I said I would look at them with an open mind.

In my research and reading I have come across several published communications that are known generically as 'channeling' or 'channeled material.' I even have several books on my bookshelf from various channeled contacts, whether they are from nearby star systems, or are classified as discarnate entities. I was open to delving into such material to see what 'words of wisdom' they may offer up. So, I made the bold step of agreeing to read some of these 'received communications.' And Nicola made the even bolder step of sending them across to me. I shortly received an email containing the first of these communications. It was at this point that I found out that Nicola had been calling the contact ABE. This was, she said, the name they had given her. Nicola didn't know herself why they chose this name; we only found out when we questioned them later on – as the reader will also find out. To begin, the first two things I realized when reading the initial ABE material was that all the messages were positive – no fear mongering or messages of doom or end of the world type of stuff. And secondly, it was quite common sense and down-to-earth, as we say. That was a good start. I immediately asked Nicola to send me some more of the communications. Nicola was still hesitant and didn't seem entirely sure if I was being truthful at this stage or coaxing her on, yet she obliged me by sending some more material that were a series of questions and answers that she had done a few years previously with a female friend of hers. Nicola had subsequently ceased with the contact. Why? I wondered. Why had Nicola not continued? So, I asked her. She told me that things were going okay, yet perhaps there was a direction, an energy lacking.

It seemed a shame to me that such an opportunity could not have been developed upon. After all, we never know where a path may lead a person, and what may open up from these pathways.

My feedback to Nicola from readings of the early ABE material was positive. ABE was speaking about maintaining our stability, our personal vibrations, and to steer towards unity. There was nothing I would consider strange, weird, or even cosmic about it. The messages focused more on trying to be a stable human being. I think Nicola was relieved that I came back to her with an encouraging response, and that I didn't consider her a weirdo and immediately cease contact. At this stage I was willing to keep my perspective open. Then Nicola ventured forth with another proposal, albeit in her timid way. Would I be interested in asking a few questions to ABE? Now, who could refuse such an offer? Not me.

And that's when it all began.

The ABE Sessions

Around late October 2018 Nicola and I agreed to meet online to do some questions for ABE. Nicola had a four-week semester break from her university studies and so it seemed a good time to put aside for focusing on the ABE contact. Since we were only in virtual contact, we thought it best to create an online document that could be shared by the both of us simultaneously. This would be a good way of being in touch with the answers as they came; and I could, if necessary, write any immediate follow-on questions (which happened often). We didn't really know where we might be heading, or what would materialize from the whole venture. Yet as they say – nothing ventured, nothing gained.

It was a Monday morning - that's all I remember. I couldn't say if it was sunny or rainy, or either what the exact date was – just late October 2018. And it began with my first question: **Hello Abe. Can you explain 'who' is Abe?**

Just who, or what, ABE is, is explained throughout these following chapters. I would also like to say that this is something which the reader shouldn't get too hung-up about. For me, the notion of communicating with the unified source field - the origin of everything before physical manifestation - is unique. It also fits well with the latest findings in the quantum sciences, as previously discussed. Yet, at the end of the day, is this really the important point? Read the communications – and if they make sense and work for you, then trust in your own innate response to the communications. That, after all, is the important bit – not *who* ABE is, but what they have to communicate to each of us. Anyway, we had to begin with a first question – so we made it a 'who' one.

Then the rest of the questions followed in what I termed as 'Setting the Scene,' as the reader will find when they arrive at the next chapter. I didn't have any specific plan in mind. Most of the questions were, admittedly, planned out in advance. I would sit down and think them out, write them down, then transfer them to the online document for the next day's ABE meet-up. Yet there were also many questions that were asked directly as follow-up ones, once having read the answer to the previous question. These were then numbered in the order they were asked and answered. All questions in the book appear in the chronological order in which they were asked.

I had decided in advance upon certain themes I wished to address, once the 'setting the scene' was out of the way. These were themes such as consciousness, health, society, technology, the cosmos, the future, etc. In this, the questions were finally divided into sections to group themes together. Over three weeks and over two hundred questions later, we felt we had come to a natural end. We felt as if we had collected a wealth of material. What we needed to do next was read through it all – again – and to try to absorb what we had been offered.

I should say a little at this point about the way Nicola works. It is the simplest method. What she does is that she reads and 'mentalizes' a question, and then receives a response in her mind. How it works, and what that voice sounds like - well, only Nicola can explain that. What Nicola writes is in a continuous flow; that is, it has no punctuation – no full stops or apparent sentences. Why this is, I don't know. I wish it wasn't this way, as it would make my life easier. After each response I need to read through and format the words into grammatical sentences. This is not easy, as it is not always apparent where the break, or pause, should go. Is there a full-stop here? Are these two separate sentences? The combinations are various. I hope I have done a good job in piecing these communications into readable constructs. If not, then most of the blame lies with me (but not all – read section below on ABE style). When the reader is going through this material, bear in mind that perhaps the sentences could have been formed in a different way. Maybe you wish to make your own grammatical combinations?

During these communications the connection between Nicola and myself developed as we had been quite literally strangers to one another - and with ABE too. Naturally, these communications created greater connection between us. ABE would say – and does say – we are all inherently connected in this way anyway; we've just forgotten this and have de-synched away from this essential connection. So, if anything, ABE is a good reminder of our communality.

And ABE has not stopped reminding us!

The Present Moment

ABE says we have become a triad – ABE, Nicola, and myself. It does seem to make for a good 'flowing' connection – and it's all about the flow. The ABE communications continue almost on a daily basis. Nicola gets her 'nudges' (as she calls them) all the time. She sits down, receives and writes, then sends them over to me and I edit, format, and archive. Whenever questions arise, I also post them on the online document and Nicola goes online and posts her replies. The connection is now more fluid, informal, yet also stronger – or rather, deeper is a better expression. And this is now how our triad is functioning.

At ABE's suggestion, we have established a physical presence – a website and social media page – where random communications can be posted, and where ABE material can be freely shared. ABE likes to refer to this as our foundation. It's not quite that yet, although we hope whatever we are able to offer will provide some form of 'coming together' and sharing for the human family.[36]

I cannot say where all this is going. Neither Nicola nor I truly know – to be honest, neither of us thought we'd even get this far. Like all good, natural things, we're just going with the flow. And, of course, trying to remain in-synch.

And now for a note on the ABE style.

A Note on the ABE style

Nicola receives the ABE communications in the form of a 'stream of consciousness' style. That is, the words are almost entirely without punctuation and consist of continuous words rather than sentences. After I receive the communications, I read through and do my best to format them into grammatical sentences. It appears that the sentence style can be somewhat 'archaic' at times. There are many 'but see,' 'but hear this,' 'see this,' and similar phrases. To be fair, these are very useful markers as they allow me to see where one sentence finishes and another one begins. There were times also when ABE seemed to say something in a way that was not the most fluid, or modern way, of saying a thing. I

36   See - www.thewaybackhome.one.

wondered if ABE wanted for me to 'translate' their communications into a more flowing, informal manner. So, we asked ABE the following question:

In the formatting of this material we have made very minor adjustments, such as punctuation. We have not interfered or altered any of the wording. We wish to stay true to this material. There are some phrases that sound a little awkward. May we change these into better English, without altering the meaning or content?

If you feel extremely strongly to do so, then yes. We would also like to say that if you are on the borderline of wanting to, then we feel it should be kept as it is. Love and Light - Abe.

There you have it – we were given permission to make alterations only if we felt 'extremely strongly' to do so. Otherwise, we were to leave it alone. Perhaps there was good reason for this. Maybe, just maybe, the transmission style of ABE is also impacting the brain as we read – acting upon our own inner cognition? I leave it to the reader to ponder more on this. For now, I have left it more or less exactly as it came forth – as it was *allowed* to be.

Another point to raise is that in these initial communications – or *allowances*, as ABE prefers to call them – most of the messages were signed off with 'Love & Light.' This may seem like a cliché in many channeled or 'new age' material. Yet the reason for this became evident in a later series of communications (not in this book). ABE later shifted the 'Love & Light' to 'Allowance & Light' as a way of showing that what we often take to be 'love' was more the romantic form. Yet for ABE, 'love' is an energy of *allowance* that is central to how all forms of consciousness relate. There is more to say on this in relation to later material. For the extracts given here, to avoid over extensive repetition, the use of 'Love & Light' has not been included throughout – only given in the opening messages. After that, we have just left the ABE moniker to sign off the communications.

A Note on Chapter Questions

Almost all the questions that appear in the following chapters are in their original chronological order of when they were asked. In this, nothing has been changed. None of the questions – or their respective answers – have been in any way altered from their original context, other than for grammatical formatting.

There are a few occasions where we received additional information on a subject that appeared at random – that is, not as part of a Q&A session but as a 'question-less' nudge that Nicola received. On these few occasions, we placed these 'extra nudges' as continuing from the answer to a related question. Yet overall, we would say that 95% of the questions in this book remain in their original positioning. That is why some questions may seem to jump about a bit in terms of their subject matter; or that we later return to an issue that came up in a previous question. The reader will do well to remember that many of these questions were formulated in advance of the scheduled Q&A sessions and so they naturally run-on without going back to clarify a previous answer. Some issues are thus returned to and clarified further in the text. Some of the questions may not be as clear as we would have liked them to be, in hindsight. Yet they reflect our own exploration as we tried to understand these experiences.

You, the reader, are experiencing the ABE communications in virtually the identical way as we first did. And we would prefer to leave it that way. And from this, the reader can find their own responses, and perhaps conclusions. Everything you read here is exactly how it came to us – isn't that good to know?

Finally, the only thing left to say is – I hope the following five chapters of ABE material will be as rewarding for the reader as it was for Nicola and myself. Read on!

Chapter Eight

Setting the Scene

1. Hello ABE. Can you explain 'who' is ABE?

We came forth as a collective of energetic form, but we very much understand that form is not classed in which your worldly physical reality is, so let us explain. I am ABE, I speak for many for in this plane of existence separation is not of essence. We are a multitude of which is not ever born into the world of physical form as you know it but understand we are very much still a part. Take it like this - you are experiencing the world in your physical form in that you have a body; this body is not separate from the whole. You are of a denser vibration in which resonates to that of your home in which you are a part of. You are in physical form which means that you are energy like us but stood still as a point of attraction; you are part of what is all motion, ever-changing but you are stagnant just for a short time. What we are, and I cannot come up with anything else that will enable us to speak of an individual consciousness for it does not exist here and it will not exist for you when this time is over. What we are is what you are and life is never apart just taking form moving through and out of form, like a candle that burns down to liquid because it has changed its physical form - does it really mean that the candle is all gone? I am able to be an 'I' for the essence of communication; to be able to come forth in such a way that will enable us to convey that which is important. That your life here is of beauty and difference and separation but here it is of collectiveness and oneness, free from conception. What we want to come forth to do is unify the two essences together to enable a humanity of divine essence, of divine being, to realise that in which you are and that in which you can become. We want to guide you to the way back home, here and now. Love and Light - ABE

2. How would you describe your location in terms of place or space?

See, we are able to have space and time and place because of you. Like an antenna that picks up radio waves they are never positionally located until a device is enabling it to be transformed. Our point of place is here at this moment but not of location at all. What is enabling us to come through is that the mind is expanding as you evolve. This will be so as to let in more and more. What we want to do too is to enable this transition - to know of it but to also help guide so that it will not be of confusion. As to what is happening, we feel that at this time there is an epidemic as people are struggling. You see, like we say you are stagnant, and you cling to this in your form. Energy is shifting you along and coming in to help flow but like a dog with a bone you will not let go. Love and Light – ABE.

3. Do you experience time? Does the concept of time have meaning for you?

Time is not a place, a point, it is really a social construct. It will never be able to be rid of as this is your human structure. From the very first part of human activity you have tried to ensure and predict and prove that I am here, and time says so. This is really the essence of time - to locate and divide and direct one thing; to slice it up into little sections. But if you think right now you will see that time is false for when can you ever trace back? It is only memory and it is so that it is happening right here and that too of your future. Knowledge that this is so then enables you to use time as it is and not how your existence has taught it to be. Love and Light - ABE

4. Would you describe yourselves as a collective consciousness that perceives as a unity? Does this mean you gain experience collectively?

Yes - we are a collective consciousness. A web of consciousness, one could say, in which through all of time and space and place; experience is woven in inter-relational, interconnected, and picked up as to what you are attuned to.

For you have your eco-systems right down to the very energy at source - your bodily eco-system, your environmental eco-system, and the cosmic eco-system all different levels, perceptions, points of place working in perfect harmony at each and every level but non-separated at all. Our connection would be that knowledge of what you are is lost. Our connection is to enable you to see this interconnection, this vastness of perceptual experience; that there is a wholeness in this separation and that which looks like discourse at one level is harmony at another. Love and Light - ABE

Let us come forth as to what true knowledge is. Philosophers all throughout time have depicted and try to understand what knowledge is. True knowledge from our standpoint is allowing that in which you are. All knowledge is knowable, it is just that you think that it has to be attained - every experience, everything, every flap of a wing, crush of a rock, birth of a child, cry of a death, are all a vibration, a part of a pattern intrinsically interwoven into a web of consciousness. All is known, everything that we know is what you know. There is no separation in this; this is really what we want to come forth to do. Take, for example, technology; it has allowed you to communicate all over the world. What you have within you is much more expansive. Each and every one is a part of this cosmic consciousness. It really is so; it is just that life has caused so many to be fixated on the known physical essence of your being and forgotten that pool of consciousness that is readily available to each and every one. When you understand this then you have knowledge. It was always there, our only advantage point to you is that we do not have the dense energy in which you call body. Love and Light – ABE.

5. How can people develop their understanding of these vibrational levels and their harmony?

You ask about the levels in which the harmony works between each and all levels. Put it like this, it is vibrationally inter-relational like the body with its environment. Although they are not apart from it, it correlates, it speaks vibrationally to one another. You have just found this out through the study of trees and its communicational pathways. Everything is talking to one another whether known or not. When unknown your vibrational essence can be hard and cruel acting upon all that is around. Even if you do not utter a word, one could say that this web is an ever-expanding web of consciousness created by vibrational essence. Harmony is only sought between these seemingly polarities when all are connected, for if the heart was cut off from the body it would not function. As so with the whole of life -communication is of essence and with correct knowledge of what that actually means is of essence. We are not to say that it should be acted upon. No, quite the contrary - harmony is not something sought out, but something allowed and opened up to. Love and Light - ABE

Our feelings towards humanity is always one of great love for how can you not love part of that in which you are for that would defeat all that we are? We are not here to say that we are above and beyond like many would like to be thought of, but we are a part of that in which you are and in which everything is. We want to show you this; to be open to the beauty of contraction and expansion. With Love and Light – ABE.

6. Has any part of the ABE collective had experience of the physical realm of existence?

Yes, all have. Like we say, this field, this pool of collectiveness is forever dipping in and out of form. Religion tries very hard to describe this as Karma. Karma would be action, like there was something that acted. But what we say is a constant becoming; we are not of body; we are not of what your mind may conceive us to be. Therefore, it is very hard to put in words this consciousness is of one but also of many. Love and Light – ABE.

7. Can you elaborate upon what types of physical existence has been experienced by the ABE collective? On this planet we call home and/or other planets?

Understanding of these levels is about vibrational alignment. To that of which you want to understand you can only ever move to that of the mechanism, the brain. To understand would be to evolve but to evolve you must first understand that you are so much more than your physical essence. That is but the starting point. For energy to experience physicality it has to have a point of attraction. This point of attraction is but the construction of the mechanism through time things have evolved. Every planet is different; every planet is vibrationally aligned with that in which it harbours. Like we say, it is inter-relational. If you are asking if there are different life forms on different planets, then we would be inclined to say that it is abundant all over the cosmos; but is a vibrational match - that is why you cannot see it. It is not recognizable in your form to be able to see. But as you evolve you will too see that the whole cosmos is alive. Love and Light – ABE.

All of life, all forms, for we can only say this because we have no form; to have no form is to be all forms and although we construct ourselves as a collective we are a collective of all consciousness - all times, all space. This is the fundamental key that all you are and what

you will ever be comes back to this. You may not
have Nicola or Kingsley as you do so now but
there will be an impression of that for you too
in this form or should we say as none for there
will always be an essence of you. You are but the
same. Love and Light – ABE.

8. Is there a part of the essence or consciousness of Nicola and Kingsley within the ABE collective?

But of course. There is no separation at all. It is
so inadvertently intertwined we are surprised
that there is even a construct that could perceive
separation at all.

It is all about vibrational alignment. But see
this, we are zero-point now. You see, all over the
cosmos life is evolving at different rates. We are
not here to hurry your species along in any way
shape or form but to assist in the energies that
are being felt. We have been to Earth many times
before and have been mistaken for aliens or spirit,
but we are neither. We are what you are evolving
to but also that in which you also came from.
Now to answer that in which we communicate
to others we only do so to assist, never to direct,
but to broaden the scope. As to the stage of what
the species are at, there are always people that are
susceptible to subtle energies, although some are
very much constricted to their physical life but
some are not and it is easy to convey with such
ones. As for the word intelligence, we would
say that it is really been over humanised for
intelligence is the way in which you collaborate
and harmonise with your environment. It really
is not something to gain but to be relational to.
Therefore, if that is so the case, then it would
be relevant to say that we communicate on all
that can vibrationally align. This is done so

by allowing flow without the stagnant self in human form, but not so in all other forms as this is not an issue. Nicola is vibrationally aligned because that signature in which you hold onto all day long is dropped. One could say that it is a falling into rather than a trying to align to. Love and Light – ABE.

9. When you use the term 'vibrational signature' are you referring to the human mind/personality – or self – that gives the vibration a particular manifestation?

It is so. It is like the paper filter - a dissolvable one, but when it is no longer in resonance with the body becomes whole again. But hear this, your laughs, your smiles, and love resonate within others. With much Love and Light – ABE.

10. You said that ABE has been to Earth many times before and have been mistaken for aliens or spirit. How did this occur if ABE is a zero-state field – did a part of ABE manifest in form?

It was never as the form of ABE, you see, but of a filtering of consciousness of which the organism is resonating at. You see, it is allowed through you and will inspire and come forth in such a way, even if somewhat constricted by the brains conditioning. Is this of understanding? You see, this is but more unlimited in a way we have been able to come through previously and this is because of evolution of the brain and the neural pathways. But see this, when there are so many pathways it will come back to but one. With Love and Light – ABE.

11. Is our evolution somehow linked together? That is, we need to harmonize our energies so if there is disruption here on Earth it will affect the evolution of the other planets?

The whole cosmos is interrelated and harmony within this system is of importance, but it is not led in the way you think and destruction to you may seem like harmony to others for your planet is always morphing to the energies available. See that human conditioning is so to be seen of doing and acting and although there is need for this there is also a time to be guided by that. Many people are resonating below that of what the planet is resonating at and therefore out of harmony. Then there are others who are resonating highly but maybe are not of the world. For your own evolution it would be wise to marry the earthly energies to be in sync with that first and foremost and to connect also with the cosmic consciousness. This is your evolutionary path at present. This would then harmonise the planet and that of the cosmos too.

12. Are there other species not of the Earth who are here in physicality in order to resonate highly to assist evolution on this planet?

No, it is but a calling of this one thing. You see, it may have been necessary before because you were not developed enough so would have come through a secondary source. But now there is no need for this as you are evolving. Is this of understanding now?

The reason you can dip into this cosmic consciousness is because you are very much a part of it but when in physical form you are entitled to block this out completely like changing the channel. You cannot hold and hear two stations at the same time, but in the future with your bodies changing to receive more and more energies then this would be possible of other species. Remember, this where we are coming from is a place of zero-state; also, your body is limited to the energies it can receive which is a good thing. At present for to go from one state to another without progression would be detrimental. It cannot be that way. ABE.

13. You state that our present evolutionary path is to connect with the earthly energies. How can we best achieve this?

Yes, it is very much so needed to be able to align yourselves to this. Firstly, many have lost touch with their environment and like the lizard whose receptor was covered up in an experiment you are lost and out of sync with your environment and when this is so, you are not functioning well. You are sick, out of balance, for to take the environment away from any species you see that their health deteriorates. So, it is of utmost importance to start resonating again to your home vibration. This is done so by that inter-connectedness, of being in nature and of bringing nature back into the system. It seems that in your earthly existence things have become very much sterile and although may be seen as good has wiped important things out that allows this relationship between home and self. Realise this - there is never a separation and what has been taught is that there is so, and in this creating a great dissonance - correlation not segregation. ABE.

14. You also state that we are morphing to the energies available. Is this how evolution occurs on this planet - by adjusting to shifting available energies? If so, what is the origin of these energies? Many people feel we are currently experiencing a transition upon this planet - is this connected to a shift in 'available' energies? Can you explain? Thank you.

The energies are available from all around the cosmos. The original state is the zero-state: the zero-state is this endless becoming of form and of no form. Life is cyclic. Evolution is very much a vibrational process but also a material one too. See it like this, a human is physical in time and space; vibration is not only felt it is transformed to that of the environment. It is so very tightly interwoven that it is hard to see a starting point within your physical existence. It is correlation and transference that allows evolution in physical form, but it is very dependent upon the energies available to it. See a toaster - the toaster is working all well and good when the mechanism is capable of transferring the available energy to be of use to something within the environment. Higher energy for the mechanism will blow the fuse and be of no good; too little and it will also not be in sync to do what it has to do. Do you see? There is a transition and like we say it has to be a process rather than a jump. To get to the home resonance is important but the next step is evolving to be more holistic. In that being the cosmos, we understand that it is very much in action as we see such energy rooted in so many. But even so the social construct in which you are within is making it difficult to enable these things to flourish and we realise there will always be a struggle to create the new. But it is turning, and it is a process. Like we say, we are not here to spread dire news but for people who are not exposed to this kind of information to see and connect to something that has long been forgotten and is engrained in the wholeness of your being. ABE.

Energies, vibration, is always available to those who are open to it. These energies are also from this state of zero, manifested into physical form because of resonance. Some people can indeed tune into other vibrations that are seemingly not present to that of the masses. See, it is their own vibrational signature that determines the syncing up of vibration. A relativity of such for relativity in the sense is a vibration syncing up or a system, a mechanism, that is able to receive such a vibration - one could say, more universal. ABE.

15. You state the importance of connecting and being in balance with Nature. Yet our governments are pushing toward further urbanization and persuading people to live in cities. Isn't this contrary to the direction we need to go in? Could this be a deliberate policy to create further disharmony upon the planet?

Of course, this is so. Maybe not so intentional although we understand some is; but lost in the ways in which have been deep rooted for so long. People and not just governments do not want to lose control never understanding that they never once had it anyway. What is damaging to your home is only damaging to oneself and most people are just not harmonised at all in this de-harmonisation - you can do nothing but spread that too. ABE.

16. You state that we are at a time where we need to be guided. Are there other intelligences guiding our evolution upon this planet or working to assist us? Could you explain more on this? Thank you.

We are happy to be connecting today. We would like to communicate firstly that yes, we are in touch with other intelligences but see it like this, we are also not separated from them either. You are very much at a young stage in evolution compared to others, so we would say that we are not communicative with so many of your species. With other species around the cosmos this is not so as they know that indeed this separation from what we are and what they are is not definitive in no way shape or form, and in this we don't come forth in the same way as what we would to you. See, life is very singular, and we come forth to you in individual form or collectiveness to communicate and get across that in which you really do know. Sometimes you need to just wake up and remember that is our purpose. ABE.

17. Is there a reason why you are communicating with us?

The reason is that you will bring these messages forth in a way that haven't been before. Your hearts are very much aligned and opened for this receiving. Not many are so in this way. In your non-egotistical open heartedness, you can receive and that is what is happening here, a clear channel, a clear heart. ABE.

The reason to communicate with you is because of again resonance. What we also would like to say is that the time is right, and people are all evolving at different rates for that is the beauty of life in all its colours and diversity. What we would also like to say is that indeed we do communicate with others but see it like this - if you are aware of this kind of thing as we know that others have come before as to convey messages of love and light you will understand that the message is loud and clear and consistent and that is of unity, of collective collaboration; maybe not in body form but of a singular consciousness, one source. There are levels of consciousness; see it like this, to be that of a Russian doll; the further in you get the smaller and smaller the space. This is so with consciousness. ABE.

18. So, you communicate to other intelligences - including ourselves - through vibrational alignment? Would you refer to this as a form of thought transference, or telepathy? Is this the fundamental form of communication in the cosmos?

Ahh telepathy, a heightened subject within your realm of existence. It is but the communication of the cosmos. But see this, it is not something that you are anticipating; no, but something in which you are to allow to open up to. See, this form of communication is not something that you are making your way to but to a way in which to remember as to that in which you have always held. You have long shut out things in which are part of your being of this world. You have many distractions and things to keep the mind occupied and stimulated but you are yet to understand the magnetic vibrational alignment form the core, the heart. Vibrational alignment is and always has been an open heart, for when this is closed off, you are not able to fully communicate. You have long been lost in language. I remind you of the saying, a good old heart-to-heart. This is, it opens; this is resonance, this is truth. ABE.

19. You say that the way of communication of the cosmos is a way we need to remember. This suggests we have fallen into a collective state of forgetfulness, or detachment? How can we move back into a state of alignment or resonance?

Yes, your planet is but in a slumber of sorts. The way to move back into alignment is to connect with each other, with the planet, with oneself. See, it has come about that relationships are dire in all aspects of life; with your beautiful home; with yourselves. There is nothing but judgement and condemning of feelings and emotions, like it is unnatural to feel and that one should toughen-up and get on with it; make something of yourself, and the relationships to each other to be that of competition. Not many show their true selves, their true feelings, through fear of the heart being broken. That they must defend it at all costs; but it is not true. The more open your heart is the more authentic your life is, and the easy life can move through you; and in this not being continually offended by others. ABE.

20. Do you have any relationship or attitude toward our species, humanity?

For isn't all just one relationship? We will say that again we are not separate so for us not to feel deeply for your species and that of your planet would be shutting a part out of which we are - then who would we be to be allowed to speak of unity if we are so splintered too? Our position is that of unified consciousness and although it seems to be that we are from another realm and something apart, this is really not so. The relationship we have is unity and for guidance from us to be able to receive comes from your own splintered mind, it is not of our separation but of yours. When this is so you see yourselves as acting upon the world or the world acting upon you. It is not - it is a collaboration of consciousness filtered down through smaller and smaller, tighter and tighter, constructs. To see the wholeness is to really be in collaboration and to be in collaboration is to be in harmony. ABE.

21. You suggest that we should 'open our hearts' and be more trusting in our emotions. Yet we live at a time of great emotional manipulation and exploitation, especially through our media. Is there a danger of becoming emotionally unstable or vulnerable if we move into our heart space?

For wouldn't it be the best time to do so when such things look so dire? Yes, people give you reason to not trust, but in the very closing down of your heart space do you not then close off to all that you are and all that you are to be? For one to be open-hearted could be said to be one of a selfish act, for you are the one that will feel life openly and honestly, therefore experiencing it in a way that is meant to be. We are not saying that you should be passive at all; an open heart is guiding and if you truly are open then you will receive much more from life. Is it not that what it is all about? ABE.

22. Since there is no separation between us, as you suggest, then in communicating with ABE humanity is actually in conversation with another aspect of itself? Is this the same as being in contact with our 'higher selves' as told in mystic traditions?

You see, the higher self has too been very much conceptualised, and even though it is an aspect of you it has been taught to be a place to aspire to in most traditions. That this higher self is meant to be of highness as suggested in the name but is not as so. One could say an aspect of that in which you are but also an aspect to that of which we are. In communication with ABE you are indeed in communication with self. We like this very much; we want you to understand that there is so much division in your realm and we use realm lightly and match this up to the analogy of the Russian doll as we would not want you to misinterpret that there is some place OTHER. ABE.

23. Have you communicated with Earth or humanity on previous occasions? Have we known you by a different name in the past?

We are always in communication with the whole of the cosmos; it is just dependable upon what is open to receive, and at what the mechanism can allow. See it like this, we have conveyed with other beings, they have conveyed with your planet through others that are open to their guidance. It is an interwoven interconnecting vibrational web of communication. ABE.

All the knowledge of the cosmos is available like a symphony, an inter-weaving of existence. Our relationship is but the same as your relationship in that it is an interaction of seemingly opposites in a world of unity. For to discover anything of your planet, like greats who have come forth and dove into this pool of knowledge before, it has to be interpreted into form. These greats of humanity did but one thing and they tapped into this, into us; they stopped trying and just allowed. You see it as when you write - if you are thinking how to do so your writing can become entangled. To truly write is to allow what wants to come forth at this present tense. ABE.

24. Is the ABE collective synonymous with Source? Has humanity in the past had contact with ABE and interpreted this as God?

Yes, is the only answer we can convey here. It was of a time of very much a singular polarity mindset in which was captured and overtaken for mass suppression of that in which you are. We feel that it should not be interpreted as God or source as these words are but too much over-used and overburdened and really get in the way of that in which is truth. ABE.

25. It may be difficult for some people to accept that the origin of life, and of religion - the Source of everything - is a zero-state field. We might get a few blank faces! Would ABE like to comment?

There will be people who are not of resonance to this, of course, and who may stare at you with a very much blank expression. But hear this, as the pathways are built in those who are of resonance they are making the vibrational connections; then the pathways will start to be built too in physical form and in physical form people will see and in this will allow these to be built internally. Is this of understanding now?

26. How would you prefer to express this concept we have as God or Source?

We would like to convey it as unity or unification to be a better word - the unification of self. Too long you have been splintered and divided. This is how things are now seen in your physical realities and have caused great pain to the masses, not only on your planet but to that of the whole cosmos. ABE.

27. How has this caused 'great pain' to the whole of the cosmos - could you please clarify?

Of the de-harmonisation and destruction waving out as a ripple throughout all of time and space.

28. Is this why there has been much activity to communicate with humanity in order for us as a species to find re-alignment and resonance?

Yes. We are here to guide and for you to see the unity in your existence and to connect you back up to that in which has be long lost. ABE.

We would also like to add that although there are cosmic repercussions from such disconnection it really needs to start at the base and that is unification to one's self. There can never be anything universally accomplished from a splintered mind. ABE.

29. There are wisdom traditions that teach a 'spiritual science' - a path of inner development - that may include certain exercises and visualizations. How does this path correlate with what ABE is saying about connecting with the unity field?

We would like to say that it does not quite correlate in a way - that a different approach is needed now. For so much has been contaminated, like a Chinese whisper that has gone around the world far too many times and now does not correlate at all to the original words first spoken. You see, it has gotten lost in translation. But hear this, you see there are not some long drawn out notions of healing within a person; it is simply coming back, a coming back to this. You see, it is but so simple that you overlook it for you think it must be drawn out for all this contamination took but so long to accumulate. But it is not so - it is an almost unity 'oh yes' and you can see and keep picking yourself up and simply bring it all back in. Is this of understanding? You see, we do not want to say that these traditions have not been of use and could possibly help someone loosen the grip in which you hold so tightly to your splintered self. But see this, you make it as easy or hard - it is but your choice. ABE.

30. In the past there have been communications with other 'collective intelligences.' Can you comment on these communications? Were they expressions of self that were intermediaries, transmitting information from Unity?

All is but an expression of this, yes. It is but one and if you were to collect this information all in one place you would see that it very much interlinks with one another. The reason in which we have come forth and have continued to do so is to take it back to the bare bones, if you will. Your species are evolving; no doubt it is seen across your planet, people waking up from the suppressed states. You see, it has been an infection of mind in that it has been too overused the way bearers will be the ones who keep their hearts open when all others want to close them off and put them under lock and key. ABE.

31. You say you have come forth. Should we interpret this to mean you have become more manifest at this time in order to assist in our understanding? Does this imply we are at a significant moment in our planetary evolution?

That is exactly as so. And this is why things can sound in contradiction, but they are really not. For something to come to form it has to be of no form first and foremost.

32. Are there currently other minds on this planet receiving direct communication from ABE?

Not in this form, no; and not of present time.

33. Why was the name 'ABE' chosen - for any significance?

ABE is significant as to what Nicola brought forth of her own being. Like we say, it is of collaboration; this was a fitting name to that of which you would say abbreviation in that we can be of contraction. Is this of understanding?

ABE was short for abbreviation: abbreviation meaning a term that is of something that is of contraction; shortened, lessened, meaning we are to put nothing into one thing as to shorten, to put a doll inside another doll.

34. You said that you have never been born into physical form, and yet you also state that your 'collectiveness is forever dipping in and out of form'. To us this sounds like a contradiction – could you clarify what you mean here?

Ahh good morning, a good question in which to start with. The contradiction you see is of course from your own standpoint and we see it as so that there is no separation. For whatever is form, we are of it - but we would never take the form as ABE or of any of the collectiveness. We are not a form - like we say, more so a pinpoint - a point of attraction than a form. So, we have never been into form, but our formlessness allows to be in all form but not of it. Is this understandable?

35. Understandably, from a human standpoint this is a difficult concept. If there are ways to clarify further, we would appreciate this. So, would a part of ABE dip into physical form, such as part of a species? Is this how universal manifestation operates?

We would like to use the analogy of the ocean and the wave, but we see that this too has been used by many. We would not be in physical form for we are specifically a point of attraction of which is being channelled. Never of form but you see what we are and what you are is not any different, so I am in form but not of this form. We are eager to answer these questions, and we thank you for your continued connection. We do feel so that this communication can move on quickly now. ABE

36. By being in material, or dense form, is life in service to the unified zero-state? What can be understood by the concept of 'service'?

We would not like it to be one of service, for you see you would be putting yourselves in a form of hierarchy of consciousness. It is but differing stages and differing views. You see, if there was one big crash of a drum and that was that, it would be but an awful waste for you wouldn't have time to dance for the moment you would of stood, the song would of been but finished. Is this of understanding?

37. There is a phrase we like. It says – 'Simplicity
is more complicated than it looks.'
The truth of our connection to Unity is simple,
yet we have complicated these matters.
What would ABE say to this?

Like just discussed, the constriction of self is
always up to you. You can resist and hold tight
to that of which you know and feel comfortable
with to continue - or you can allow much more.
Is this of understanding? You see, simple is
always hard for you in human form. For you
see that if it is simple and comes easy then it is
of no importance. You know that this is not true
at all, for life should flow. You clearly need to
participate in this life but life does not have to be
battled with, just met. ABE.

38. For millennia, humanity has talked about
spirituality and the spirit. We have long searched
for spiritual understanding. Is spirituality as
simple as connection to the unity zero-field and
allowing pure consciousness?

We would like you to see not as but a connection
in a sense that you have to get up, plug in, and
be of doing - but rather an allowance of. For if
you are having to connect up in some sense,
then you have simply lost the notion of it all
together. It is but an allowance of it - to breathe,
settle down, and allow. Is this of understanding
of how spirituality is? For we would like to say
that you are already spiritual, for you have just
forgotten about your vibratory essence and
connection to all. It is really a remembrance. It is
but an understanding of what your heart already
feels and picks up. Do you see? ABE.

39. So, the big question (and we have to ask it!) - what 'is' the meaning of life? What are we here for?

For the whole meaning of life is to live, and to live one must be allowing of all that you are. For to not understand that you are but of physical content but also of vibrational too, you are but living a half-hearted existence. But we think you have gotten the notion of this, so we will put it like so: meaning of life is you. There is no particular meaning that all of life should abide by. But hear this, meaning in life does so get lost when one is very splintered for it feels like the whole world has taken a piece of you and you are but lost within the noise outside of yourselves. You see, we would not want to wipe the whole world clean, void of expression, for the meaning of life - if it is to be of anything - is this EXPRESSION of but one thing. For you see, there would never be a dance of life if one had to do it all alone. ABE.

Chapter Nine
Mind, Body & Spirit

1. We often use the term 'God', yet this is misleading. What is your understanding of 'Divine Source'?

Ahh yes God, the word that has caused so much hatred in your world when all was to be seen was the complete opposite. You see, we have come forth for this reason; because we do so indeed see that like we said, things need to be stripped back to the bare bones and this is so with your understanding of the divine and also of God. People are of course free to choose in that of which they do wish so but for the ones who are not drawn to any of these terms, and we do so feel there to be many now, we want to say that God, Divine, universe, source, are all but one thing and you are it. ABE.

2. Have earthly religions been successful in representing the Unification/Source?

We see that they have, and we are not saying that they have not served a purpose at a different stage of your evolution. What we are saying is that to move forward now these outdated ideas are not going to serve you well to see the whole picture. They are not so much to be rid of or dismissed, you would not say to your mother 'oh well, you gave birth to me a long time ago, you are of no use now,' for we are in a large cycle in which some point you will come back to the beginning and this will be the forever becoming. There is truth in all religion, but it seems that these things are driving humanity in the complete opposite direction to that of which it was intended to do so. This source or collective or God is that in which you are - how could it be any other? You have been sleeping and it is time to wake up to that in which you are, which everything is. We know that a lot of new age movements are saying that we are all one and this is true unification, but we feel that they miss it out that this is also science; it is also God; it is also every terminology that could be ever thought of. You can never dismiss others, and people will always have their own beliefs - but what we want you to see, to truly see, and not just that but feel - in the core essence of your being - that even in this world of great polarity I see you in me and me so in that. ABE.

3. To return to Source - is this what you mean by *the way back home*? Could you clarify what you mean by this term?

The way back home is really first and foremost back to the home vibration being your planet, and to be aligned with that for we feel it to be too much of a step to go from low to resonating high with the planet. This step cannot be skipped; what we also say is that to do so you have to unify. Within a split consciousness of 'me and the world' is never going to be able to see to it that you are a transactional vibratory essence that is not separated from your world - more so, an expression of it. This is not to say that you do not impress upon the world either, for you alter vibration by that at which you resonate - so it is always transactional. So, to be unified it would be to see and wholeheartedly feel that you are transactional, that you are whole. ABE.

4. How would you regard humanity's current spiritual state? Has our species had higher knowledge previously that was lost to us?

There have always been stages at which your species have been higher developed spiritually, but still it has been tainted by something outside of yourselves, that being of a God. The state of your own planet's spiritual evolution is progressing rapidly and has been so. That is why you see more and more destruction because of the fighting to keep the old. What we would like to say that there does not have to be a choice; just a knowing; a wholehearted feeling that what we are stating is truth - not because we say it to be but that you feel it deep in the core of you and resonates with you on all levels. ABE.

5. You have said previously that the state of our own planet's spiritual evolution is progressing rapidly. Does that imply that the planet is a conscious organism? Is the Earth also in communication with ABE? Could you clarify this?

Good morning both. We are delighted to clarify but a few things, and feel it is of importance to do so. You see, it is so; but one could say that also the Earth and all differing planets are of a constricted consciousness. By that, of its own vibrational signature and to that that is upon it and also around it. You see, like we say about the pathways - within and also it is also so without. You have your connectors within the brain that create neural pathways due to vibrational resonance and this is so with your Earth. Now hear this, as your planet evolves and morphs and changes it will resonate differently and like your internal self will also create differing pathways too. Is this of understanding now?

6. There have been many 'wisdom traditions' operating upon this planet. Did they have access to Source, to the Truth? Did you have direct contact with any of them?

Like we say, it would not of been of the ABE form; but we do believe that people have had this connection even unknowingly so. For some people, they are inclined to have this type of brain functioning in which they never lose this connection albeit how hard they try to shut it out throughout their lives. And there are others whom through evolutionary processes seem to have developed a masking of this connection and the brain develops differently. But this is not to be said that it is not available to them. One could compare it to, say, more so of a deeper sleep. ABE.

7. There have been many spiritual Masters upon our planet. Were these ordinary people who gained access to the Unification energy, or a deliberate material manifestation of consciousness?

But of course, we would like to tell you that all who have ever walked your planet have had this connection to unification energy. But also, too, it would be a deliberate material manifestation of consciousness because it would have come forth in such a way as this. ABE.

8. Are there other terms that have been used/are in use that may help to clarify the ABE state?

The one who has come closest would be that of Zen tradition; and we understand that you have to name things in your world of polarities. Zen too in a way has become tainted for it is seen as people taking themselves apart from the world which it is not, but this is now tied to the word Zen and people see it that they would have to give up all that they love. The only way is to be of it and in it; there is no truth up on the hilltops but here in the midst of it all, in the polarities of existence, knowing that it is all quite ordinary but seemingly extraordinary all at the same time. ABE.

9. Is true science a knowledge of vibration? If so, will we arrive at this knowledge?

We feel that indeed science is a knowledge of this vibration. But it can never be truth in the sense they can measure and record with seemingly pinpoint accuracy. But it is always going to have to compare things and always have polarity. In this you will find marvellous ways to be in your world; advancements and knowledge of it. We are never to dismiss this for it is who you are too. You are human beings of your world, but it will have to always measure and dice and slice and in that will not have the full picture. What we see though would be something of a merging. If science can see the completeness and the undivided essence of life within their boxing things up, truly see it - and we are sure it is already going in such a way - then that would be of essence. ABE.

10. Is vibration at the core of our health? How can we heal ourselves with the knowledge of vibration?

Vibration is a core essence of health care, for vibration is the language of life. For you to be out of vibrational alignment of your very own being, if you are split, then you are creating discourse within the body. Everything has a vibrational signature, so it is true with that in which you put into your body for that is what tells the body what the outside world is like - if it is thriving or not. So, it has to be of great importance that you are 1. aware of the vibrations of the things you put into your body and 2. that of your own vibrational signature. You see, this too is inter-relational. You could have all the best food and eat well and exercise but if your own vibrational essence is that of lack that you are eating this nutritious food, then you are no better off than eating all the junk in the world. For you see, there are people who are extremely fit in the world and have health problems because they are not aligned with their own vibration and that in which they are putting into their bodies. Is this of understanding?

11. Is certain healing knowledge being deliberately withheld from us? If so, why is this?

I think it would be of both. See it like this, there are people on your planet who know of these things and are keeping them alive within their communities. Indigenous people pass this down through the ages by ways of ritual. What has been done, that more so in the west, life has been pushed in such a way that this knowledge is seen as new age or mystical, that logical reasoning and science can be the only way. What we would like to say is that there is also a dissonance in this and if unified with the so-called mystical and that of science then medication will be a thing of the past. But you see, your very system has been built on such grounds now and will be difficult to re-establish without a fight of someone wanting to hold on to some sort of past. You see, it is never about one better than the other but about the merging of both - the unification in things. ABE.

12. What will be the future of human health? Will our health systems be forced to change?

The future of health really does lie in the people's way of change for they too need to shift and let go of past habits that do not serve them. You see, you know in yourselves and your bodies when something is off if you are attuned to your being, and you would know how to nurture your body back to equilibrium. But we are not saying that you need to be dismissing that which is of your physical world and science, reason and logic, for they are intertwined aspects of who you are and how you experience life as a human being. It is in the emergence of both that the key to health really lies, but we feel that both sides will find it hard to let go of their deep-seated beliefs at first. But it will happen. ABE.

13. What will be the future evolution of the human body?

The future evolution of the body will not be of the body but be that more so on the consciousness level. Not so much on the physical to start with but as the consciousness of your being rises, or one should say resonates, the body has to adjust too to the higher vibration in which way the body will not be so dense; it will not be so heavy. ABE.

14. Is this evolution of the body to a lighter form a natural evolution that occurs in all dense matter as it develops? Has this bodily evolution occurred before on this planet? On other planets?

It is a natural progression for they would not be in resonance. But see this, for you to become and be of this world there has to be some kind of density that is also resonance to that of your home Earth. This would be subject to all species and you will then see that really you do resonate on a physical level. It can be no other way. See, what we have now is what many people speak of as the love vibration that being of the cosmos and this is true in a way. We want you to see that there is an expansion coming, evolutionary, that will enable your species to expand in consciousness to that in which we are. But hear this, it will always be of a density to match that of your planet. It can be no other way, and this is so with others. ABE.

15. As the human body becomes less dense to resonate with an altered consciousness, then how will this relate to the physicality of the planet and other species upon it? Will there be a similar shift in their density too?

Yes, it will. But see this, they will be subtle changes overtime and never a leap as you see it has always been so, and will always be, of harmonisation to all that is, of the planet too. Is this of understanding? It is always inter-relational, and you will not be of such lightness or transparency with that of your planet Earth for it is rather dense in its vibrational essence, albeit shifting. ABE.

16. How do you mean we 'will not be of such lightness or transparency with that of your planet Earth for it is rather dense' - will humans not be 'of the earth' in this time, or that the Earth will not shift in the same way as human bodies?

No, you will but shift to that of the planet for you cannot outgrow it at present. For the purpose of conscious evolution at this time is to put deep roots into your planet. Is this of understanding? But hear this, for if the planet is making other connections and is not at all of resonance to that of its beings, then they will grow increasingly uncomfortable upon it. Do you see this?

17. What is the importance of food and diet for human health and awareness? Can you say something about the current state of our food systems?

It is important in the way that it is inter-relational to that of your own vibration. Like a sock in the wash that is dominant in colour it will colour all that is mingled within it. So, it is important. Like we say, it allows the body to sense what the outside world is like - a vibrational communication system. The current state is that it has been far way taken from its own harmonious balance to that of the Earth. To see that your Earth is suffering is to see that you yourselves are also suffering. You are creating a dissonance of vibrational communication through the toxins and chemicals that are being used at present and, in this, creating a cognitive dissonance. ABE.

18. Does a contaminated vibrational signature affect the food we eat and vice versa?

Always it does - it is but transactional. See it like this, someone who but knows no other than being that of their own vibrational signature are quite dominant in a sense to get their point across. Someone who may be not so caught up in it are not so and are seen as introverted or shy. But hear this, they are but allowing – see, it has been the dominant that has been cheered on for so long but in this you have gotten too caught up in this game. And we may have strayed again, but you see the dominant force lords it over and therefore whatever is not allowing to meet and be of benefit to the system is not going to be one of health or of nourishment. Is this of understanding?

19. What is consciousness? How does this function with the human body/mind?

Consciousness is the signature of form but also that in which it comes from. It is this. See this again with the analogy of the Russian dolls - there is consciousness, then there is the doll. This is form. Then there is another doll - another form. And inside that, another doll, until you come back around and there is consciousness again - space emptiness, one could say. Although space nor emptiness is ever void. You see, consciousness is always at a point of attraction to that of the mechanism, or should I say organism. To be pure consciousness is to be void of form completely. See, we have no form; therefore, we can be everywhere within all form but not of it. This is hard for your brain to conceive for it is always working within the parameters of polarity. It is about the essence, the knowing of this form and allowing consciousness to have a more fluid flow. Is this understandable?

We would also like to add that mind is not consciousness - it is your unique vibrational essence.

20. Our histories, our experiences, etc – do these help to develop each particular aspect of consciousness? When each vibrational essence, or consciousness, returns to no-form (ABE) does it retain any sense of individuality within the collective?

This is but a fine line. See it like this, a toaster which has the electricity running through it but when thrown away or broken beyond repair it is unplugged. You see, there is no obvious notion that it left or imprinted the electricity upon this one thing. But hear this, like we have mentioned before, it is a joining up for the evolution is not of just you, no, but that of the whole cosmos. To answer more direct, there is not a specific part of you that is in the shape of you. But you see, there is but a web of consciousness - to be one of connection not of form at all. But you see, it is a vibrational pattern that can be tapped into, almost like a membrane. Is this of understanding? But please, do hear this - it is never of two separate things, just a filtering through as such. ABE.

21. Our minds – or vibrational signature – also reflects our personalities. Could you clarify the relationship between consciousness and our individual selves?

It is but a filter in a sense. But see this, it is not two distinct things - but we do so feel that we have to explain as such. In your world of polarity, it is but always in and of itself despite the separateness you do so feel at times. It is a change of vibration in which to bring into form that of which you resonate of. Is this of understanding now?

22. How is consciousness linked to evolution upon our planet and within the human species?

Consciousness is what we are. See, we are only a point of attraction; because of the brain this then creates the vibrational signature you see as mind. Mind is not a part of consciousness; it is a part of that which is body. It is the unseen signature, your vibrational signature, that speaks in

vibrational terms and resonates. Consciousness
is devoid of form - it is zero point. Mind is not
consciousness but your vibrational language
back to consciousness. Is this understandable?

When mind is dropped, when you do not cling
to that of your vibrational signature or self, pure
consciousness is allowed to flow.

**23. So human ego is blocking the flow of pure
consciousness? Does this suggest that we should
detach from our personalities in order to allow
connection with pure consciousness?**

You can never but detach - it's about meeting in
the middle. In the knowing of it as unification,
never a one or the other. But hear this, it may be
of a good notion to but put it down and see - to
rest without trying to uphold it as you do. ABE.

**24. And how would this flow of consciousness be
linked to human evolution? Is it also somehow
linked to the evolution of this planet? That is,
can we participate consciously with our planet's
evolution?**

Yes, that is so. In the allowing of consciousness
to flow you are allowing life to move. We know
you hear this now as more of a Buddhist view
but what we want to say is that consciousness
should flow, yes, but you should also be able
to unite matter with this. This is where your
evolutionary key is - there is no way at all that
this energy will not be influenced in some
vibrational way in your existence. It cannot be
so, this is life, but in the allowance of it, it will

really propel you forward as a species. Realise this though, we do not want any species to be void for what would be the point of that? ABE.

25. How would you suggest for humans to develop their minds? Are there any specific practices, such as meditation?

Mediation is great but sometimes can get caught up with escaping here to be in your body. To be feeling all this to be a part of all there is and also to be able to know the expansive truth too whilst here in physical matter – wow, what an experience. What a life. Be with it, feel it from the centre of your being, and most importantly – participate. ABE.

26. It is said that the human being has an organ of perception that can be further developed. Some traditions say this is necessary for our evolution as a species. Can you comment on this?

This is to be so of the pineal gland. There was an experiment a while ago which I think we may of mentioned previously, about a reptile that had this sensory organ connected to perception covered up and struggled to read it's environment. What we would like to say is that it had been of importance in a way. See it as this, you are a blind man of the world and you realise that driving may be off of the agenda. You still are able to sense the world with your stick or dog. See, the dog becomes an extension of your sensory apparatus, enabling to help you navigate the world. But if you had your eyes back you would not need this. This pineal gland has been beneficial in the past, when your brains were not so developed, but are not necessary for the way the brain is developing now. Just like everything else, the vibrations enable life to be pieced together and harmoniously intertwined in a way that you could never imagine. ABE.

We would like to say and end today by saying that you are all in control of your own each and individual evolutionary signature. That is being human, and in life sometimes it causes you to be bitter and resentful and closed off from this web of vibrational communication that is now being spun right from the very first thread. It will always be contained within consciousness and therefore the more united it becomes the more this vibrational essence of each and everything harmonises. The more available it is to you, all vibrational alignment, this web of communication will infinitely expand. ABE

27. You have said that some people's brains develop differently, and so block out their natural connections. Has social conditioning within some of our cultures been a deliberate attempt to wire human brains in such a way as to keep people in slumber, so to speak?

This is indeed so. For like we said before, how would they be able to sell your parts back to you if they do not firstly recondition and break it apart in the first place? For you see, it is a game of life in which you have been coaxed into playing and in this you have thought that it is indeed what life is all about. But this is not true, there is so much more to it. It is just that the wiring is all wrong - you see this? You also have to remember your parts in it too, for you have been hypnotized by the highs of modern-day society and when coming back to this it all seems rather dull, rather un-special. But you will see that the one who is awake will indeed see the extraordinary within the ordinary. We know that this is not included within the question, but we would see for it to fit. You see, the DEPRESSION epidemic is one of dissonance because people feel torn between vibrational alignment and the rewiring of the vibrational alignments of the brain. In this you see that now too depression can be a false premise to keep you in this game also, for it will be nurtured and hung around in far too long. Is this of understanding as we know that we may have strayed considerably? ABE.

28. Thank you, ABE. Yes, this is important. If social conditioning is a deliberate attempt to keep people unaware, or in slumber, then is it because there are those in power who understand the truth - the truth of what is ABE and of our connection to Unity-Source? Or is it only because slumbering minds are easier for social management and control?

It is so that people are to use this power in a way to manipulate, and it is also so that people are set - they are not at all interested in getting out of their seats for they have all that they need right here, do they not? Why question it? For you have enough food, even if it is not right for you and the system, but that doesn't matter for you have the little pill to fix it too and in this a great dissonance and a great disservice to all that you are. For some will go an entire lifetime and have never lived a single true moment in their entire life. What a shame. What a waste. ABE.

29. How and why do we experience love?

Ahh, good morning. We see that this is of importance here to convey. Love is a vibration felt by the heart and directed and labelled by the mind or vibrational signature. You see, all vibrations are felt; they are then filtered through mind or vibrational signature. Your own unique vibrational signature transforms a vibration into a thing; as it is transmuted by it, it is transformed so then that love vibration which was felt say between people was pure consciousness flowing but you labelled it and made it a point of attraction or pinned it upon a certain person or thing. You see, the vibrational signature holds it all; see it like this, you start off with a large lump of clay - we will call it unity or unification or consciousness - you then want to play and make separate things holding it to account with experience. These are the vibrational signatures, what we would like to say is to realise it may seem like different things, but it is still just one thing that being clay. What we would also like to say is that it is not a bad thing to love people and we know in your world that love is very conditioned, where love in reality is unconditioned. It flows, feel it but don't direct it; don't mould the clay and tie it to things and people. ABE.

30. But what about our world of relationships?

We see that this can be confusing. For you would say, if we love all in a way that no-one gets special treatment, that you do not have close intimate relationships, then you will be destined to be alone. But we do realise that you have a circle in which you are in close proximity. We would never say to not love them in a way that you do. But to know that what you love in them can be extended to a stranger on the other side of the planet and not have to be so contained. It does not have to say that you should love everyone in a way you love your husband or child, but to see that there is no difference in the love that you feel on the transference of it. See, the more you have open-hearted communication and connection with others you realise that you can do nothing but love them. ABE.

31. Why do I not love others and then feel stronger for another?

You see that your vibrational signature can cut this off through past experience. This love is in constant flow, constant motion, when the heart is open but as we say, your vibrational signature wants to open and close and transfers it, filters it through past experience in a way as to protect the organism. You see a person you have all the vibrational conditions and you either allow it or block it. You then match these now feelings to that person or place or thing which in reality was only a memory or a belief and like we say, you let it flow or you allow. ABE.

We would like to add that you see that some people give their love freely to others and some do not. It is all about that vibrational signature. You see, when you first fall in love you are forming this connection. It is allowing universal energy to flow between you unrestricted because you do not yet have any conditions of this love, this connection. As time goes on, you experience more of life together and you bank things in the vibrational signature bank. It gets cluttered and love is not able to flow; it gets stuck within these patterns transferred. What we would like to add is that you can love without possession and love without conditions - you just have to see that. ABE.

32. You discuss love and consciousness as vibrations, and about inter-relationality of all humans. Yet how can we make this knowledge 'real' for people? How can this information help people to live better lives? What can we do?

First and foremost, it is of importance to be human - that is it and that is what we would like to get across. Humans have flaws and accepting them is a way to resonate higher. See, what people think of your so-called enlightened ones is that they have reached a different place, and it is not true at all. The gurus know this; this is why you see so many Buddhist monks smiling, for they see this simplicity of being and how much people struggle because they think that they have to be somewhere higher, that this is not enough. What we say is that it is all here and only the splintered mind cannot see. We would never see to it that you drop your vibrational signature, and we fully understand that this is so ingrained in your experience. What you can really see is that you are not it - you are a long track of vibrations and matter and endless cycles of life and form. In that seeing, in that very knowing, how can one really be splintered? How can one honestly say that they are me and you are you? It cannot be so, and when this is seen as clear as day then, well, you will feel no need to be anywhere other than here, basking in life's undivided beauty. You will do nothing but radiate love and connection for it is all within and therefore will be all around. ABE.

33. Have humans distorted the love energy/ vibration in our physical existence? How should it be used? Have human civilizations made use of it differently at other times?

You must see that all vibration is distorted in some way or another in your physical existence - it can be no other way. Like a light that hits an object and bounces off in other directions, it is so with vibration. Now see this, though your own vibrational signature is but built with many differing vibrations, resonating to make one like water that passes through a sieve - whole, separated and whole again, this is so. The pure stream of consciousness flows through the body, through the brain, and is transformed by its conditioned state, by the vibrations that it holds, it is interlinked and also attached too: it is your vibrational signature. We understand that this seems like all individual things, but it is not so. What we are really trying to say is yes, the vibration is always changed by our own vibrational signature. What we are saying is, if you can allow it to flow - and this is done by allowing universal flow - in a way of direct experience of life. See it like this, to have the pure water you would not need a filter; it would not help. The filter may have contaminants that may affect the water which is already pure and in this being more a hindrance. So why not drop the filter, allow pure consciousness to flow by cutting out the unnecessary middleman. This does not mean to be pushed around and passive, but to have direct experience with life. Feel it, be in it, open up your hearts to allow its love. See, in your human form there have and will always be people who try to manipulate this energy flow in a way for self-preservation. But it cannot be done for if it is open heartedly flowing, then you are having direct experience with life. You see the patterns and the self is there but a part of this whole. The only people that know of this and want to manipulate this are the ones who push for self-preservation. ABE.

34. You have stated that ABE is 'zero point.' Does this mean that the ABE collective consciousness is the prime energy that is the source of all things? Is ABE where all physical consciousness manifests from and returns to? Is there anything 'beyond' ABE?

This is so, that we are where all form is and where all form is born from and will eventually fall back too. There is nothing beyond this because there is nothing. For in the nothing you hold everything; it is within the spaces of things that you really have life for. You see this within all your music and language - if there were no space there would be no life. ABE.

35. We all share the same consciousness - we are ABE and ABE is us. We are aspects of ABE in material - or dense vibratory - formation. Is this correct?

That is correct, and we like to keep going back to the Russian doll analogy for it shows that you and only you restrict this flow by means of being engrained and engrossed by the vibrational signature. Hypnotized by all its goings on, treading carefully as not to offend or hurt this vibrational essence; but in the seeing that it is just this it can be let up. ABE.

36. If our consciousnesses are intertwined, then is it possible that you know our questions before we ask them? It is like having a conversation between ourselves?

One could say that yes, for that is how we would see it. Like the whole universe is mad, talking to oneself. But you see, you also do have this vibrational signature for a reason too - for that being there can be a myriad of expressions of just one thing. How wonderful that is to see - we do not say get rid of this but rather allow more in by letting it up. You have become so frightened by it in a way, and in the knowing that it is not really what I am; and 'I am' is a lot more expansive and inclusive. You can realize that life isn't so terrifying, but a great expression of one thing and you can go ahead and just live, just participate. ABE.

37. Is all human thinking a process of receiving/ tapping into this collective consciousness? Is this what is meant by inspiration – what the Greeks called the Muses?

It is so, for when you open up the doll you allow space to flow. It is not another within another but believe us when we say that you are opening up the dolls and are not putting them back together. People are letting up on this vibration but only fear keeps you restricted, for in the fear of loss of self that you will not exist. This has been a vibration from the beginning of time that humans want to say that 'I were here' and that 'I existed' and here is the proof because 'I am me,' but what they do not see is that it is a false identity and if they just let this go a little they will see that there is so much more to be open to, so much more to be receiving. ABE.

38. When artists such as writers or inventors receive their ideas, are they transmitting ideas from the collective consciousness field? If so, is it not the case that ideas have been seeded through such channels to help to evolve human civilization?

These are great questions and we feel that there need not to be such drawn out answers from us for we see that you are of great understanding for you are very allowing of this flow. For in your own work you have but help open minds and create foundations for evolutionary steps forward. We have a question to you - how does one feel when writing of these things? Do you feel yourself, or that you are allowing something other? ABE.

39. As an example, popular science-fiction books and films are sometimes used to manifest and distribute ideas for later possible actualization?

This is true, for sometimes it is great to get a message across by a song or a film or a book for this widens the scope to which people are touched by these things. See it like this, as in the previous question, the whole universe talking to itself to be able to know itself. These things set in motion as little pointers to wake you up like alarm clocks dotted all about the universe. ABE.

40. How does this relate to Carl Jung's theory of the collective unconscious?

Very well, for was he not just doing the same and bringing this universal consciousness into being through his own vibrational signature and in this he let up on his own vibrational signature to allow that of the one consciousness to flow? ABE.

41. You have previously stated that 'there are others who are resonating highly but maybe are not of the world.' Could you clarify what you mean by this?

We would mean so in the term of not your world, and of the planets you are yet to discover. See, all is at differing evolutionary stages, and this is of harmony. ABE.

42. Does ABE distinguish itself from other communications that have been 'channelled'?

To us we would feel like this is and has been of use to those whom seek that way. But for us it is really of being human - we do not want to take you to our being for what would be the point? But it is more so of a seeing and realization of how great and wonderful it really is to be in form. There have been so many that have tried to take you away from this by trying to reach a higher state. What we feel is that it now needs to be grounded and brought right back down to Earth for it really to be of any use to humanity. ABE.

43. Many traditions talk about 'higher consciousness' – what they really mean is a rise in the resonance of one's vibrational signature? Is this rise coming to everyone as part of natural evolution? Is there a method whereby a person could individually accelerate this vibrational shift?

Good morning, we are happy to have this continued connection with you both. Higher consciousness is indeed that way, not a higher place to get to but a resonance in which you are more accustomed to be - more open to receive. Now see here, we do not mean for a person to have to resonate at a certain point like you really have to do anything. It is of the notion of coming to grips with that in which you are. There is never anywhere to get to, just a knowing of that this is how it is. Now if you are asking as to move this along more quickly, then it is really just in the allowance of this knowledge; really getting to realize and understand that this is how it is so - by truly experiencing it and done by allowing it to flow. ABE.

44. What is the role of DNA within human evolution? Is it also a vibrational code? What is the function of the majority of unknown DNA once referred to as 'junk DNA?'

Ah yes, it does indeed make us laugh at the word junk for is it not in the knowing that something to be of use and is now not? Well, this is not so; it is just that your sciences indeed are not able at this point of your evolution to decode that at which they are not open to. You see, the more open you are to this flow, these vibrations, the more you let go of your very constricting conscious mind. You know that when you let up a little space you allow something to move and in this you are able to not only understand but clearly see. Your DNA is very much the vibrational code of life - it is vibrational memory. Like we discussed earlier, one big conversation going on but to itself. One could see it like this: you have your parent's vibrational signature and through this you create and wind these two seemingly different vibrations and create a new vibration. This is but the structure of your DNA. ABE.

45. In our physical reality right now there are a lot of problems with obesity and food-related illnesses. There are also an unprecedented amount of chemicals in our food production. Are we creating greater dissonance with our bodies?

But of course, this is so for you are trying to control and conquer something you do not have the whole picture of. For if you really could understand yourselves then you would indeed not want to put the things you do so into your bodies. The harmony of the body cannot leave out that of your environment in its natural state. For you are mixing up the vibrational alignment by trying to straighten it all. But you see, you do not need to do so for in the straightening out of a wiggly line you are flatlined. You kill it - do you see that this so makes sense?

46. What can you say about the rise of genetically modified food sources? Some people consider them our future - should they be introduced into our food systems?

We see that there are many people on your planet and believe that as this continues to grow there will be more of a need for growth in your food production. What you do not see is that by making these modifications to your food you are indeed making these modifications to your planet and in turn the cosmos - it is always inter-relational. There will always be ways in which life will cause you as a human species to modify life, to upgrade to solve, and this is indeed good. But in the seemingly extreme concentration on one area you automatically denounce another. It needs to be more open and understanding of these vibrational essences of life and the inter-relational connection of everything. For if this is understood clearly you can do nothing but automatically move forward and in this flourish. ABE.

47. How important is physical exercise? Should we know our bodies better? Practices such as yoga are popular now – are these good ways to develop body alignment and resonance?

Mm, yes; see exercise as so an interaction of seemingly two separate things. You see, your ancestors moved all day long until it was time to not do so; and we know that advancement in technology has caused many to be very stagnant and still. A lot of times throughout the day in this you are not allowing this energy to flow; you are not connected, for when you are stagnant it is so that energy is stagnant. This actually slows down and lowers your vibrational signature. See this, though no movement is better than any other it is purely just movement needed if your vibrational signature is matched to that. To do yoga - by all means do that. You will indeed get much from it, but if it is not so then it will be of no use VIBRATIONALLY. See, we discussed this resonance earlier with you talking about food and then your being is begrudging of not having a different food. As such, it may well be good for the mechanics of the body, but the vibrational alignment will be out of whack. Health will never be healthy until you take on board that you are also very much a vibrational being. You can take care of the mechanics, but you also need to take care of your vibrational signature. This meaning, you also take on the vibrational signature of that in which you eat. We are not denouncing these great ways of getting people moving as they do indeed also make people aware of their own energy etc. What we are saying, that no one is better than any other form of movement providing you are aware that you are also vibrational. ABE.

48. Greater numbers of people are suffering from addictions, especially alcohol and drug related. How are these issues related with the times we are living in?

They are in a way to escape this - that you have been so tightly focused on self and how and what you should be doing and being that you look out on a world that is tough and disconnected and lonely. You see, all these things do, really, are allowing you to drop you in a way. You are not that, and many people know this, but society is saying you have to uphold this idea of you, or you will not survive. You will not succeed, and the dissonance is caused and when dissonance is caused you want to escape this. It is so very sad but so true, and we are not saying that you should feel sorry for people who use drugs or alcohol, for there are many who do not so but are maybe obsessed with changing lovers or addicted to food or sex or working. See, anything can be an addiction in a sense, to escape this life. I suppose it is just what people are going to choose as their vice. ABE.

49. Diseases such as cancer have increased dramatically in recent years. Why is this?

We can say but two words and that is - vibrational dissonance. We feel so very strongly to convey this at this time as we see it ravaging the body of many, taking countless lives. It always starts off as dissonance, always. ABE.

50. There is a lack of understanding about death in our modern societies. It feels as if we need to see it as a transition stage rather than as the end. What are your comments on this?

See, death will always be so that it is hard to grasp, and of mourning for many who do not understand the part of that in which you are. Clearly, you have some emotional attachment to say of a dear friend or of a loved one. It will always be so, and you would need to let that vibrational part of you come up and express for there is never any sense in pushing it down. You do not need to become unattached to life. You see, in the beauty of that heartfelt release of another, you feel alive. That is beauty, that is part of being human. What we would like to say that this is not the end. It is of the body as it cannot continue, but your vibrational signature is always in the mix, always. It is like making a cake: many ingredients make up on thing a cake. That is what we can say as to life after death. You see, people saying that they have a near-death experience and they may well see a light, for the signature is still there; it is still running through, but it is still very much a human thing. When you have no body you are no longer splintered - you are back to wholeness, that is it. ABE.

51. Continuing the theme of understanding the end-of-life transition. Could you say something about the process that occurs after the death of the physical body?

The end of your body is not the end of life, just a change in form, for you always go back to the whole. What we really want you to see in your human form is that you are a cycle; that you are this wholeness. There is deep beauty in this process. There has been much fear around death, and it is understandable in a way as your mind works in the polarities of life. You see, this vibrational essence of who you are is a part of this wholeness. It is not soul - you do not leave the body. The body changes form. The vibrational signature that was once blank in a sense, or zero, is now going back to the pool of pure consciousness. Life is a process and there are always different stages. The vibrational signature does not leave, it just hasn't the bodily resonation to sustain it, for it to be stagnant, so it returns back to the source. But hear this, it does not become lost. It is a collection, but not of physicality, like a soul - a wholeness in life or consciousness constantly expressing itself, constantly talking to itself. Does this explain it well?

52. What can you say about the concept of reincarnation? Do particular vibrational signatures return to form to continue with life experiences?

One could say that you have all lived every life for it would be silly to say that wholeness or oneness has not lived all lives - so this is of truth. What we would like to say is that there are also resonation of the vibrational signature. You see, your religion is very much based upon a physical entity of sorts that would lord upon man to be good and moral, so religion imposed the idea of a cycle coming back and back until you finally get it right. There is some truth in a sense that life is cyclic, but no truth in that it is to get this life right. You see, that is very much a human concept; for if you are not thriving in this life surely you could then be in the other world. But there is no other world, and to some this can be disheartening. There is just one world in different expressions and that one world is the whole thing - the whole show, for it cannot be any other way. So, we wanted to express to you that if there was a matching of vibration, one would see this as the soul cycling around and around. But it is not the continuance of a person to another, for an essence of your passed ones is in the world, in everything. There are specific signatures that attract signatures of another type, but it is not of you going into another body neatly packaged to live again. It is not this way at all but essence. Some might think that with this information humans would be lost but it is not so, for you will fully see that all is of you and that there is no definition. ABE.

53. Why does vibrational consciousness come or 'birth' into form? Are we here to have specific lessons or experiences?

Life moves, life cycles, life is change and life is consciousness. We would like to say that although religion and society has taught you in a way that you are here for lessons or experiences, it is not this way. You see, the thing that you call soul does not have to reach a higher state for it to be accepted with open arms and to say 'good job.' No, the overall point of all of this, the whole point of us being here, is to wake you up to that of which you already are. You are an expression of one complete thing, so to say. That you are here for lessons would in some way say that you are not already what you are. Here is a little story: a baby kangaroo abandoned by his mother was taken in by a pack of hyenas. Now all was good and well until one day the grown kangaroo bumped into another kangaroo. The other kangaroo hopped off and the kangaroo was in awe of this creature. He went about trying to be like the kangaroo but could not be, until one day the hyenas came clean and he was told that he too was a kangaroo like the one he had seen and in that moment of knowing he was able to hop and jump just like the others. You see, it isn't about lessons - it is more so about remembrance, like connecting back up the phone line that you had left off the hook. Again, so you are connected to all that you are. You see, you always have everything you need - you just need to see that. ABE.

54. Could you explain if there is a difference between what we call pure consciousness, soul, and spirit?

No, all but the one same thing - and we would be even reluctant to call it anything other than this zero-state. But do hear this, soul and spirit are that too of vibrational signature. But you see, that they are but one thing - albeit the row of identical flowers that each have their own scent. Is this of understanding?

55. You have said that disease is a result of vibrational dissonance. Could you explain more on this?

Vibrational dissonance is when two vibrations are rejecting or repelling each other. They are not harmonizing; they are not attracting each other BUT also there are more dominant vibrations. Say, a heavier vibration, a denser vibration compared to something that is just okay. See this, when you walk into a room and there has been an argument you feel the density in that room. You feel as though your whole being is weighted upon - this is the true meaning of dark energy. So, in regards to disease, dissonance is caused by two seemingly different vibrations trying to be held at the same time. Take it like this, you hate broccoli. You had a bad experience and was extremely sick when you were a child eating some. Now the doctor comes along and says that broccoli is the only thing that will make you better today. You have complete vibrational dissonance. See, life as you experience it and in this your own vibrational signature is being wound together. The body always wants to work in harmony, always, but it does that by vibration; by talking to each part vibrationally. This vibration is and always needs to be in resonance to that of which you are, and also that of your environment. But you see, it is not so. For example, you could eat something that is factory made, that is dead. In a way it is vibrationally talking to the cells, to communicate that in which your environment is like. In this, the vibrational signature will be lowered because it tells the cells to act in a certain way. But see this, if you are eating only organic food and your own internal vibration is not a match to this, this also creates dissonance. There was a lady whom only ate fresh organic fruits and vegetables, never smoked or drank, exercised regularly, and still died at the age of 35 from a heart attack. This was because her vibrational dissonance was caused by the vibrational signature she had due to her heartache. She was so focused on her health and wellbeing she forgotten about her relationships, and in this she felt that dissonance in her heart. Life is always about balance - always. ABE.

56. You state that DNA is the vibrational code of life. Could you explain more about the role of DNA? Also, how does DNA relate with consciousness? Will human science come to work more with the properties of human DNA - and how?

DNA is the building blocks of life, it is true. For in this vibrational code you have all the knowledge of who you are. You see many new age groups saying that you can wake up your DNA for the codes for activation of higher consciousness, and this is true. But see this, it only carries what is up to now, and presuming that you are not fully evolved then you can see that there is point at which you will get right back to here. But see this, DNA is also a receiver of vibrational code, so you are creating new vibrational code by your own being. You contain vibrational code from that of which you have come and evolved from, but also you can receive new DNA structure by opening up to this one consciousness. As you see, this is evolution; this is the way in which your species allows itself to take the steps forward. Is this of understanding?

57. You have said that humans can receive new DNA structure as part of their evolution. Is this similar to, say, receiving a new program 'update' that provides new information for developing? Could you say more on this?

It is in the creation of these pathways so it is but put into the program to pass on a memory bank of evolution. Is this of understanding? For when new DNA is then created it is binding together what is two resonances and creating but one new and one could say and hopefully would be improved, evolved. Hear this though, it is also a receiver of what is. ABE.

58. You stated that 'many new age groups saying that you can wake up your DNA for the codes for activation of higher consciousness' and this is true - up to a point. Could you clarify more on this? Thank you.

It is true in a way that you can awaken that in which has been and what is already present. It is not true to awaken pure consciousness. You do not need to activate it but allow this vibration. In this you see, it is molding together past, present, and future ancestry vibration - your vibration and that of pure consciousness. Is this of understanding?

59. In that case, is it really necessary to have New Age groups performing these rituals like a service? Can we not allow this activation/flow ourselves through our own intention? Is there a personal method for this?

This is what we want you to see. It is a very human condition to put power outside of yourself. There really is no need for this - it is indeed through your own knowing. You really do have to start to pick up the pieces that have always set you apart and really start putting this cosmic puzzle back together to wholeness. We are in no way denouncing these practices for they do awaken people to be more open, but many get so caught up in it. ABE.

60. Is DNA the code of life for the cosmos? If so, how does DNA function for other planets and other species?

You see also that DNA resonates and picks up your vibrational code. It's like a get together of past, present, and future, and then deciding what to build its foundations on. It is the code of life on all planets and works exactly the same for all species all over the cosmos. ABE.

61. How did DNA originate? Was it 'developed' in some way?

DNA is but the code of life, the building blocks in physical form to pass on that at what stage you are but at. As you are moving into less of a physical evolution and more so of a conscious one, you will see that DNA is also a receiver of vibration enabling it to be built and to bring together that which resonates, an attraction of such. For from the very first building block was born but from the one thing but enabled it to become split and in this it was breaking down into smaller and smaller parts, marrying parts together through resonation. For the first whisper of life it was born into be that something of separation. But you see, it was not just an expression, a dance of life. Is this of understanding?

62. In terms of bodily health, is it expected that human life spans are going to increase as part of our future evolution?

This will be so, for your life span is always increasing due to the technological advances and the more complex the brain becomes. You see, these vibrations create new neural pathways, new connections, and in this building a new structure. This means you will become more complex. Your bodies will not be so dense as the vibrational essence rises on your planet, and in this will allow the system to thrive for longer. But see this, technology will be a large part of your futures. You will have morphed in a way to be part machine and this will work, say, when you lose a limb or something dramatic happens to the body - it is of use then. What we would like to say is that in this vibrational evolution, this one of consciousness, it will be evident that you will live longer, for the body will not be so pressured - the vibrational signature will not be so dense. ABE.

63. Human sexuality in terms of gender roles seems to be shifting, and blurring. Many people are finding that to be either 'male' or 'female' does not fit into their physical and psychological well-being. Is this related to our current evolutionary shifts? Could you comment on this?

Ahh, we see this and would like to say but one thing - social conditioning. For in the splitting of say more and more genders you are but casting the net of more separation. The people who do not classify that they are but one or the other are so just saying 'I am human, and love is love and this is it.' We see that things get lost - why not be that of being human? ABE.

Chapter Ten
Human Society & Culture

1. What is your knowledge and perspective upon our history here on this planet?

But of course, every vibrational signature, every experience, has come back to this. But hear this, you know all that is - you are able to always tap into this knowledge by allowing it to flow by unification. We are not something outside of you. Take, for example, the Wizard of Oz, the great old wise wizard of Emerald City, knower of all. But honestly, when you pull back the veil, just a normal man. You only limit yourselves by shutting out that in which you are. For if it is not of substance then it does not exist. Tell us, what does it mean to you to exist?

If you are but asking us to reel off history, then we can say this - there has been great famine, destruction, cities found and lost, civilizations come and go, and this will be so again. Your planet and the cosmos are in constant flux, and the ones who resist and hold so tightly to what they believe, and cannot move forward with this, will surely not be able to keep their own heads above water due to the new vibrations, due to this new energy. We say new in a sense of that it is new to your form right now. This is what has happened before, and it will surely continue. ABE.

2.Thank you. You say we need to keep our head above water due to the new vibrations. What can you tell us about these 'new vibrations?' Are we going to experience a period of increased disruption?

We say new in a sense that it is new to your physical bodies of this time and space. We would like to say that these vibrations and energies are manifesting at great intensity and there will be ones that fight hand and tooth to keep things the way they are now. You see, when the seed is cracked open it could be seen as completely destructive, when in essence it is bringing new life. For the new life to come forth, the old shell that contained this new life will have to crack open and this will be extremely destructive. For the more this energy is brought forth, or we prefer 'allowed,' you are tapping it in and grounding it down into this reality. In this, it will shake away all that has been built, and in this you will see that the ones who cannot walk this path will not be able to succeed. ABE.

To answer if there is increased disruption, we would say yes; as there are many that are grounding this vibration. They are unifying this of us and that of you, so the more people do this the more it will be destructive for the systems in place now. When you see more disruption, you will know that more people are enabling unification. ABE.

3. Are there ways in which people could better 'ground' this vibration and new energy? How can people consciously assist in allowing this energy vibration in?

The unification: by knowing what you are, not allowing too much baggage, too many human conditions. Our very work is to show you that you are it; that there is not a stagnant self that lords upon the world but a process of life - a united field of existence. If we can get this across to as many as possible; if they feel it in their very essence and truly deeply embody this truth, then wow - change will manifest in even the darkest of corners and it will light up all that is still hiding in the shadows. ABE.

4. We would like to assist your work too. Please indicate to us how we can best do this. Is it good for us to continue with our questions - does this assist the process?

It does assist very well, as we feel these are very appropriate to the things that people will ask and want to know; and we feel that sometimes we denounce or dismiss. But this is from a place of pure love and not to be of 'I know' and 'you do not' for we state that all this is what you are. It is really to loosen the grips you have and although you are very much loose in your grip, your mind gets lost in the language - in the naming and pinpointing of particular things. What we would like you to truly feel is this. Tell us, what allows for your inspiration to flow, for you to feel connected?

5. Some traditions have a cyclic understanding of development, such as the Vedic Yuga cycles. They say we pass from an Iron Age to a Golden Age. Could you comment on this understanding?

There will always be cycles, and we believe there are many names for this. With the one you state in your question we understand to be of an already established structure. We are not to denounce your structures and your beliefs but to loosen the grip. See, you get so very lost in language; naming this, making it stagnant, pinpointing, separating. Our basis is always unification. If this can fit into the idea that you have for unification, then it is of use. If not, dismiss it. ABE.

6. Some theories state that planetary evolution occurs according to electromagnetic cycles, or other cosmic energy cycles. What can you say about this?

We will always state that this is true - but to what notion do you have of cycles? It is built upon structures of old that have so much baggage tied to them. For life is really cyclic; you know this, you are forever becoming but never getting to see things. Never stop and start, just change, interact, morph, but never a specific time or place. Science does like to pinpoint a cause and effect. But you see, when you pinpoint one interaction you forget about the others that have led it to this, and then to the ones before. Does this answer this?

7. What would be a more correct way to consider evolution upon this planet? How are humanity a part of this evolutionary process?

We would say that evolution is always vibratory. We go back to the Russian doll analogy. For you to have your own planetary evolution, it has a knock-on effect to other places in the cosmos. And for their evolution it is also the same for you; it is so tightly inter-woven that to pinpoint this evolutionary process you would have to go right back to unification. And to see the end result, you would see also unification; and in this you can see the pattern of the forever becoming. Can you not?

8. Can humans delay or interfere with the planet's evolution, or is it out of our hands? Current thinking says that we are disturbing evolution (climate change) or advancing it (geo-engineering). Yet isn't this hubris?

There is a very fine line to tread here. We would like to say yes, you can interfere, but not so much in a way of physical action. It needs to be of this conscious, this vibratory action. You see, there will be many who will denounce this knowledge just so that they can be active in the world - active being in the physical sense. And although we see a time to be in action, we also see the need to be from no action; for you to then take the correction from a place of truth - your truth. ABE.

9. It has been said that for the past ten thousand years we have had the possibility for conscious evolution - that is, our species evolution can move ahead through deliberate, conscious, directed effort. Can you comment on this?

You see, to have something conscious, now you really have to allow. Being conscious is the key to this unification. It is an allowing of pure consciousness to be present in this time-space reality. It is who you are. We don't expect you to slay your vibrational signature or dismiss it at all, for this is also the creative essence of consciousness. It is about bringing together the two. You see, your unconsciousness is your vibrational signature and when you are not conscious it runs the show. But by being conscious, you allow these two to unify; not ridding of any one, just allowing what you are and what you think you are to exist in this time-space. But see this, they are never not flowing; but you can be unaware and lost in the unconscious, never knowing that there is so much more to your being. Does this answer the above?'

10. So, what you are saying is that by allowing pure consciousness to flow through us and into our reality - onto the planet - we are assisting with the evolutionary process. We don't need to struggle to assist evolution. On the contrary, we should learn to allow it all to flow and to ground it? To use an analogy, the human species is like a vibratory, resonating membrane - or skin - for the planet?

You need to stop resisting evolution. Stating this is not how it is meant to look. You see, this theme is in much of your life. By allowing, you sync up with the knowing that your way is not necessarily the right way. ABE.

11. So, what you are saying is that by allowing pure consciousness to flow through us and onto the planet we are assisting with the evolutionary process?

That is but so. You are, but not distorting it so much but see this - like light hitting any physical thing it will bounce off in all directions expressing in different ways. This is so, but true of this too. ABE.

12. As all planetary evolution is interwoven, would it not be disastrous for the cosmos if humans destroyed or greatly damaged the Earth, such as through nuclear war?

Oh, but of course. For unification does not hold place for war. For in the unification knowledge, you understand that what you do is only but done upon you. ABE.

13. The phenomenon of crop circles has intrigued many people. There is the hypothesis that these are messages being given to us to help our understanding. Could you comment on this phenomenon?

Ahh, the crop circles. Now see this, there have always been signals, interventions, for we live in a unified field of consciousness. There will always be pointers, and symbolism has been used throughout the whole cosmos. And although you may not understand it, it can be decoded. We would be more inclined to think that it has come from a human tapping into or being of this energy source, rather than a little green man flying in. You see, it takes a lot for other species to enter your dense atmosphere; and even more so, for they do not want to be seen to interfere physically as to impose or direct. Is this of understanding?

14. Many areas of the planet are known as sacred sites or 'energy' sites - such as Stonehenge in the UK. Did our ancestors have specific knowledge of cosmic energy? Could you say more about Earth's energy sites or energy lines?

There are such sites. But hear this, they are no more sacred than your back yard. You can tap into this anywhere. There was in your earlier conscious evolution specific points, and only because they built up the intention to connect in a certain spot did it become a portal or a place to connect. You see, if what we are saying is true - that all is unified - then how can it not be here and there and wherever you go?

15. You say that such sacred sites are no more sacred than our back yard. This is good to know. Yet what about certain energetic 'hot spots' – such as sacred buildings (Alhambra, meditation halls or tekkias) – that are said to connect and facilitate energy flow. Are these places not more conducive to the flow of pure consciousness?

No, they are not at all. They may have this sense that they are, so people are to believe that it is so and therefore build up intention of it being so. It can be felt because of the people and the resonance of connection, not because of the place. ABE.

16. What can you say about energy lines that crisscross the planet? Some of these are well-known and may be pilgrim routes. Others are said to connect specific places. Are these not like planetary neural connections?

Like we said, it could be so likened to that, yes. They are of but conscious communication talking of and to itself - vibrational resonance, a membrane as such. Is this of understanding?

17. Have other intelligences, or species, been involved with assisting the evolution of this planet? If so, in what ways? Has there been knowing human collaboration with other intelligences? Why is this subject so taboo in our societies?

It is so taboo for you do not understand yourselves. It would be spoken of if you could so get to a place whereas you knew all that you are. For in the knowing of oneself, you are knowing that of which you are. If you know this, then you can see that it is all a part of you, and it would not have so much fear. For humans think that they have to impose their way only because they are not consciously aware. But do you honestly think that other species that are more evolved think in this way? It is not so. If you are asking if other species have assisted, it has only been when people have opened up to this, an intention if you will. ABE.

18. Developed societies have entered an accelerated phase of materialism and consumption. This is stimulated by corporate greed. Is this a sign of our old systems and will this pass? Did other civilizations also pass through a phase of intense materialism?

Your existence, like we say, is one of cyclic motion. It is but an outdated system of consumerism; but understand, it will never be completely rid of it for even in the waking up to this there will always be a form of consumption in human nature. You are right to say that it has been completely monopolized by some that are based in greed. But this too is balancing itself. Your job is to be awake and conscious of it. Now there have always been civilizations that have taken too much, and in this, resources dwindle. What happens is that the Earth will bring it back to balance. Really, all you need to be is aware - the planet knows its own balance like you do with your own body, if you are aware. We would like to add that yes, humans find a resource and they take it and they see that it is beneficial and in this it is monetized. And although this is not true for how other civilizations conducted their affairs, it is still in some sense of truth. But you see, it does balance itself back out when people awaken and connect. ABE.

19. The population on the planet has accelerated dramatically within the last century. We will reach 9 or 10 billion people by 2050. There are some fears of over-population. Is this accelerated population part of our current development? Some people are worried about this. What is your perspective?

Over-population is always of keen interest. Look at it like this, if the soil is fertile you would have a good crop. You need space between these crops, so they are able to truly flourish, to be able to maximize the growth of the plant. You see, when over-population occurs the space is clearly getting smaller; your cities are built higher and your countryside is expanded, and land is taken to accommodate more people. We always come back to it, but balance is key, and people to resources is of essence. When you upset this balance by, like you say, over-population you are putting these crops closer together. You are manufacturing foods that are not built for consumption. Everything becomes quick and more, and in this a great dissonance is served. It really is a knock-on effect, a cycle, and you are it. We would also like to state that as life spans of humans expands this will also cause problems in regards to your population. You see, with this kind of problem there is no obvious solution other than restrictions in place formed by society. But we would like to say but one thing - this new energy that is upon your civilization has to resonate to that of the system. If not, you will not be able to go forward in this physical existence. This is all we would like to say on this for now. ABE.

20. Our political systems are largely corrupt, and people are losing their trust and respect in them. We are due for a dramatic change. Is this part of the necessary transformation required upon this planet at this time?

It is. As more and more people awaken, they will see that indeed things are not in balance, are off. Like you have been so conditioned in a way as more and more people come back round, in a sense they will see. But see this, people will be outraged and disappointed and angry like they have been betrayed and hypnotized and befooled, and you will see all this mayhem and pushing back. You know, we like to say that you can never fight the old by fighting it. You are keeping it there in prominent position. What does the person who wants to force their way always want? It is a reaction, a resistance, an argument but that will not solve the matter. We really want you to claim all yourselves back before you can take a step forwards - to action this is our purpose and it is also yours. ABE.

21. The global finance system seems to be a manipulated and 'rigged' system that favours the specialist financial players. Yet the flow of money is also an important system of energetic exchange. What can you say about this?

It is an important energetic exchange and has always been so, albeit in many different forms over time. We would say that this exchange is coming to an end of physical money as you know it. You will be going forward with a digital currency in which you can see firmly taking place and rooting as we speak. There will be people who claim more and channel it in a way so that it benefits a few manipulating and directing this system. But you see, as more people get wise to this, the more they can claim it back. You see, many coming together is a lot more powerful than the one holding the bunch of notes alone. They will not have power or place to manipulate if people unite. That is why they push to keep things splintered, people disconnected. A united nation is a powerful force. ABE.

22. There is a lot of talk now about digital currency - it can be used for greater transparency as well as greater control. Will digital currency not just replace the old system and maintain the same inequalities and struggles?

Not if people are awake for it can be directed in a sense as to barter, to exchange goods for goods, not to accumulate and take stock of. It just will not be in the sense as what currency is now. It cannot continue this way. ABE.

Our whole stripping back to basics is for us an un-conditioning of what you have for so long seen yourselves to be. Because other humans have placed them upon you, it is time to in a sense break free from the hysteria and come back to oneself - if you are ever able to unite. ABE.

23. There are many people who view that the world is really governed by a small group of elites who are holding on to their power. Can people really make a change through their individual efforts or consciousness?

Like we say, it is not something that can be fought. You see this with many things now. But hear this - people are waking up but are also falling into another trap of consumerism and political disconnection, thinking that always they have to pick a side when there is no side to pick and all is worn out. Then you may see, but we are coming forth to hopefully make you see a lot sooner. For if left too late, everything else will have been completely exhausted. ABE.

24. At this current time our societies are becoming more authoritarian and controlling – especially through technology. Are we moving more toward control societies? Will this not cause conflict with the free flow and expression of consciousness?

Someone who is not awake will always want to control, for if a person is truly awake, and we mean truly, they will feel no need for domination whatsoever. Now, to say if you are moving forward to a more controlled society the answer could be yes. But you see, in this suppression, this pressing something down, it will at some point have no other choice but to bounce back. ABE.

25. Propaganda and forms of social conditioning seem to be very high and there are great efforts directed into this. At the same time, you speak about individual power within each of us. How do you view this situation?

You see, it is like this; a tug-of-war pushing and pulling, always trying to get the little knotted red line to the centre of the line. You see, we are not saying that life should be euphoric, and it should be likened to that of heaven. If there is a heaven then it is here with you now, and the same with hell. You see, you are human and there are interactions and individual vibrational signatures and much more. What we want you to see as clear as day is that in which you truly are. Truly take it all back, all those feelers that state you are this and you need that and on and on - such a tiresome existence. It is in the realization that 'oh I am here, and I am also that but I can be this' - and share it. Isn't that an existence? Isn't that the true beauty of a human life? Society does indeed dumb you down and cut you into so many pieces for if it didn't so, then how would they be able to sell you your fragments back? ABE.

26. You have stated that we need to realize that we are everything – we are 'it.' Yet is this really enough to create change within our societies? To know something does not always result in tangible internal transformation.

The transformation will only come when you realize this. For if you do not break such a constricted pattern of being, then how will you ever see any change? We are never saying to not act but acting from the same patterns are never going to create different results. There will never be change and you see this in many of your worldly affairs. ABE.

27. The majority of people upon this planet have not yet 'awakened' to the truth. They prefer to watch television, or play their games. Do you see this situation changing? Will the newer energies arriving on this planet create some dissonance here?

Yes, it will, for it is like there is something in the air - like a nice smell of say fresh baked bread and they see that 'oh I am in life again.' They start to feel and shake off the monotony of just being and start living. But see this, it is much easier to sit back down and numb-out again because people are so afraid to feel, to love, and to live. What a shame! If only they knew that, wow, this is what I can do - I feel hurt but in this I am alive,

I am here, I am participating. Such beauty in this realization. ABE.

28. Our technologies now connect us across the globe. We are communicating like never before. Would you say the Internet is a reflection of our own internal connectivity? How do you envision the development of the Internet?

It is a physical adaptation of that in which you are. It is showing you in physical form to unite, to communicate, to interact. The same as when the phone was invented - it had the same effect, bringing this energy that no-one could conceive at all and putting it into your physical existence for you to believe it and use it. Now, for people who are able to adapt to this new energy or allowance there will not be such a need for these physical technologies. It is some time off, but you as humans will be connecting and allowing this flow of communication. See this, the heart is the connector vibrationally and the head is the receiver - just like a phone line. If these are both open to receive then it will be that way. ABE.

29. It seems that upon this planet humanity is evolving toward a planetary civilization. Is this so? Does this suggest we are moving toward a world government? Is this shift to greater centralization a part of the civilizing pattern, and has this occurred on other planets?

We would like to see this movement towards a united government, yes. But see this, we have said before that even you, as your own vibrational essence, does not need to be rid of it, is truly, truly in the undoubtable knowing of unification. If this is so, then we would hope that there would be no need to be governments but just humans. It has happened on other planets; but you see, they are a different species and different formations and have resonated different from the start so have not conducted things the same. They too have made mistakes and are in no way superior, just more evolved. ABE.

30. Human societies place many layers of social conditioning upon their citizens. People adopt belief systems, ideologies, etc. Are you saying it is necessary to de-condition ourselves, and if so how might we go about this?

Good morning both - we are pleased to see this continued connection. Your human society is but built upon social conditioning. It really does take you further down the rabbit hole. Its outdated structure is just that – outdated. It does not and will not resonate with the new wave, the new vibration. This is why things can look destructive for in the holding onto old outdated structures, one tends to get aggravated and at dissonance. You see, this new vibration people are feeling like we said 'the winds of change' but they are not sure what it is. This is where we would like to come in and lend a helping hand or more, so both in physical form, this connection - these words - will resonate with many, for we wanted to get it down to the bare bones again, no nonsense. The way to de-condition is by needs of allowing this flow of energy. Allowing the heart to open and allowing the mind to be free. This will take work, for hearts have become closed and also that of minds, which you know is your vibrational signature. Loosen the grip on the story of 'me' and try to allow the story of 'we' - of unity. ABE.

31. Human civilization on this planet is currently at the phase of nation states and nation-blocks. Yet isn't this a limited stage that we need to supersede and isn't nationalism a limiting vibration-pattern? Could you comment on this?

But of course. It is as we said above, people feel this need to hang onto something, to grab a hold of their identity. Some tie it to their country, some to their football team. See, people live a lot in fear - in fear that people will take what they have, their status, their belongings, their identity. When they feel threatened in this way they fight back and want to claim what is rightfully theirs. See it like this, your media puts a spanner in the works; by the end of this the whole factory is shut down wanting to never see a spanner in their factory ever again! What they do not realize is that the spanner contributes, and it was put there in such a way as to cause aggravation and separation. Is this of understanding of what we try to put to you?

32. There is a growing trend toward increased urban living – larger cities and more mega-cities. We feel that there should be a balance and more rural living. Is it not important to cultivate agrarian lifestyles and to live off the land?

See this, in an ideal world people would be more self-sufficient, cultivating the land and going off-grid. But you see, many people are not wanting to take this route. They like their cities and cafe's and hustle and bustle. What you can create though in these places are more natural spots, more open spaces: roof top farming, a box on the window, community projects, connection to each other and the world around. For this would be of great benefit and you see people coming together again already doing such things. In the Second World War supplies were limited, people were taught to work their land again, cultivating what they have, growing what they could. This was forced upon people and although we do not like the idea of directing, we do feel that there will be a time in which this will be implemented again due to population spikes. ABE.

33. Should more people consider living 'off-grid' – that is, more independent and sustainable lifestyles? Is this a good future direction despite it going contrary to current trends?

It would be, yes. But we would like to see it more community focused for it not only gives connection to your world but to each other - working together, cultivating together, sharing the food. For the best meal of the day is really the one shared with those you love, is it not? ABE.

34. Despite our high levels of connectivity, more people are becoming strangers to their neighbours. Does not the sense of unification also apply to our human communities? Will current trends not also trigger a rise in alternative communities?

Yes, this is the way we see it going - for in unification you cannot but move into a more community focused setting. People would say that they would not feel good to be in a commune, but it will not exactly be like that. More so, a gathering of communities working together. You will see this far more so when your currency that you have now is no longer of use. You see, people think that in this sense of doing this you will be taking a step backwards. But it is not so. There will be deeper connection in this to your world, to each other, and also to that of your instinctual human nature. You cannot shut out that in which you are - and believe us when we say you have been running away from this truth for some time now, through fear of stagnation and no progression. But this also is a falsity. ABE.

35. Heart communication is a strong vibration and creates harmonic resonance. What social or cultural activities would help to promote this harmonic resonance?

Connection – open-hearted connection - this is only implemented when you drop the vibrational signature, the conditioning. See it like a heavy bag that disallows you to open your arms and embrace life. For when you put it down, not get rid but stop trying to uphold it, you feel your arms free to embrace life and each other. This is the way of the open heart and this is when true connections are made. ABE.

36. Are sporting activities a form of developing teamwork and harmonic resonance? Has sport been used on this planet as a channel, or vehicle, for promoting higher vibrations amongst our species?

It is in a way, yes. Team work is important, but you see it is still quite limiting in a sense that even though society has built teams it still separates by way of stating my team is better than your team, and in that sense you are not better off at all. The idea is one of a global team, and although it sounds euphoric it is not. The one cause that all can be working towards and what you all share is humanity. ABE.

37. Our cultures promote values of competition, conquest, and control. We sense that we need our vibrational influence to shift to values of collaboration, communication, and compassion. Will these values be more dominant in our younger and upcoming generations?

Yes, but of course. They are born into this vibration. It is so different for these - they will be the way-bearers if allowed to do so, guided and not suppressed by their peers. You see the younger taking a stance, not fearful of dominant structures. This is good - this is change. ABE.

38. There have been major migrations of people across the planet in recent years. This cultural mix of diversity has many advantages, and yet it instills fear in many people also. Does not diversity and inter-mixing help to strengthen the collective human vibration in a positive way?

Yes, it does. For you are all but the same, but society can install this division and in this deepen the route of separation. For if this was not so, their structures would fall instantly. They would have no grounds, for they are all built upon the shaky foundations of identity of separation. For if you are all just in conversation to one thing - to yourself - then are you not only trying to point out that I am right, and I am also wrong? It is pure madness - it is a disease of mind, of your vibrational signature. ABE.

39. We need to bring the sense of the sacred back into our lives. The sense of enchantment and cosmic communion. How can we realize this amongst humanity?

First, recognize your humanity. For when you realize what you truly are, you are humbled. For in the opening up to that of which you are, you realize one thing - that all is the same. There is deep unification in this being - feel right back to this, right back to the core; back to the essence: the life that flows through your veins, the love that opens your heart, the ever-growing knowledge of existence that pulsates and opens up the vibrational signature to so much more. In seeing this unification, you will not be able to restrict your being again. To see that in which it once was, growth is inevitable and in this humanity is taking a big conscious step forward into a new world. A new way, fearless and open to life. ABE.

40. It is said that modern life is making us more isolated and more tribal despite our increased connections. How can we change this situation?

We see that you are not to go back in time to a set of isolated communities but a whole network. This is much like the worldwide web but in physicality - a united network of communication all over the planet and this will then expand. One could liken it to say your individual brains creating another unified brain being that of the planet - then of being of the cosmos. The neural pathways are created by vibrational resonance, and so within is also that without. Is this of understanding now?

41. Talking of alternative communities - will it not be vital to find alternative means of localized energy? Do you envision communities moving away from global-grid energy supplies? Isn't this a necessity?

Yes, this is what the work of the community is to be - to become self-sufficient. Clearly, not everyone at the start will envision this. But once they come back to unity, when they are less splintered, hear that we say, for it will be an ongoing evolution like everything else. But being amongst and working together in these communities will only strengthen that in which you truly know - that all is but one. When you see that this way of living can only allow you to thrive, then more and more will join in this new way of being. There are such better ways to harvest your energy on this planet and these communities will do so. They will lead the way in new ways, not only working more in harmony but bringing you back to life - to be able to feel and embrace it again. Finally, you will breathe again. ABE.

42. Alternative communities have existed in the past, and some still do today. Yet many have been corrupted by greed, egos, power, etc. Can you say more about how you would envision correct relations to exist within and between balanced communities.

It always will have to come back to this for you to go forward - it is like being lost on a path trying to find the way out then someone will come along and forget also within the distraction of actually being lost. What you have to do is come back to this, knowing first and foremost, otherwise you are but running around in a panic as to what to do and where to go. Stop, realign and readjust. Now, how we envision you to but go about your relations with another; well, that would never be of us to say. For you need to do so this first and then see how it feels; for in this knowing it will be of natural essence to connect. You see, you have but hid yourselves away and gone within - it is but time now to shine, quietly whispering to the ones whom are lost 'I think I know a way out.' ABE.

43. There are some communities who prefer the 'simple life' – living sustainably, sometimes with minimal or no technology, living close to the earth. Many of these are good, honest people who prefer to live away from the noise and distractions. Do you feel these communities will grow in popularity? Are these good examples of how to live in today's cluttered and distracting world?

We just said previously that you are but hidden from the world and we see that it has been of benefit. And like we say about the guru on the top of the hill, we would like it to be seen that you share and communicate and interact and but be in life with the new skills and the new ways and ideas. To share this in which you have learnt whilst taking the necessary time to disconnect - not a shouting off the rooftops or preaching but of a whisper to the ones who want but something else, something real. Is this of understanding? See this, implement the what you call the worldwide web in reality, make these vibrational contacts, these new pathways. ABE.

We so but want to say also it is not a bad thing to go off and disconnect so long as you at some point come back online. You see this?

Chapter Eleven

Science & Technology

Hello ABE and thank you for the continued
connection. We appreciate this communication.
Now we would like to ask you questions
concerning the themes of science and
technology.

1. Our science says that our known material
universe began with an event they call 'The
Big Bang.' How accurate is that? How was the
universe created?

Good morning. We are also delighted to have
this continued communication. Ah, the big bang
- a starting point at which all came into creation.
Let me ask you, do you see existence in such a
way that there had to be a point of attraction at
where it all began? For if all is of one thing then
where can you possibly pinpoint a certain point
at which it all began? We understand that science
has come to this conclusion as they want to see
a prominent starting point, but they are also
forgetting that what would actually cause this
big bang. See it as this, there is vibration, call it a
sound, and there are instruments now to receive
this vibration and interpret it in any way as such
as the mechanism is built. You see, to have a big

bang there had to be some sort of starting point at which all came into creation and although this is true in a sense for your physical world it is not true in a vibrational sense and that in what you truly are. See, if you want to get down to the nitty gritty and see the tiny details then you will honestly see that there is space and nothing and within this nothing there is everything and you see that you come from nothing, you play in a world of everything, and then you return to nothing. We are by no means saying that the big bang did not happen and created worlds, but you see it is not the beginning and there will never be a neat little packaged end for this timeline - that you do so hold onto in your physical existence is not so but a circle, a constant becoming. ABE.

2. Our scientists talk about the visible universe, yet the cosmos is a harmonious and complex system larger than the visible universe. Can you say something about the cosmos and its processes of creation?

Yes, we can. It is one of connection, of interaction and, like you say, harmonious interrelationships of this one vibration, being transformed into worlds and living beings and stars and planets. You are able to feel love from outside of yourself but all this time just this one thing, this one vibration, spread out experiencing all things across all created timelines and structures and languages. For in this oneness there is everything and although it looks like nothing in a physical sense it contains it all. You see, at the beginning - and we use this term very, very loosely but so that you can see that in which we want to get across - if in your sciences now you can grasp that beyond even energy it is vibration. That this is source, that this vibration was the beginning of it all. You see, there was never a big bang in a sense for there were no ears to hear that it was; but of itself, like something that turned itself inside out to allow these things to spill from it. For you see, vibration is of nothing - can you grasp it? You can certainly feel it for you have this physical body to sense in such a way, but you cannot hold it and you will never contain it. The more it spreads, the more it creates and interacts and connects and changes. But see this, it is all but one thing - one truth, one vibration, and you are it. ABE.

3. When we say that other universes exist within other dimensions, are we saying that they exist within a different vibrational state? How do multiverses form, and how do they relate?

It is so this way. Multidimensional is just a term for multi vibrations in which you are incapable of experiencing for in your physical existence you have this point. But see this, you are in a sea of vibratory communication; your body would be over stimulated and burn out quickly if it could sense this all at the same time. This is why evolution is key. It is a slowing down of what you already are - like a fine wine to be sipped and enjoyed and revelled in - to be fully immersed in the experience. Does this answer your question?

4. If we could shift our vibrational resonance would we be able to gain access to other multi-vibrational realities?

Yes. But see this, it will not flood in; more so, a revealing of the pathway - so long as you can keep taking vibrational steps forward, in trust of that which will come before you. Is this of understanding now?

5. Our science now agrees on the theory of quantum energy. The quantum plenum, or zero state, is said to be the formless energy field from which the universe manifests. Isn't this quantum zero state also ABE?

It is so this way. But hear this - it is also you.

6. If we are also a part of this zero-state then we have access to incredible energy. How may we manifest this energy - and is this part of our in-form function?

You are able to harness this energy as you evolve, and you evolve by allowing this energy also. It is a transactional interaction, for the energy always has to be equal to the mechanism. It is just this so, for if you draw in too much you will blow the fuse so to speak. ABE.

7.   Quantum science appears to be the science of the future and understanding of quantum field effects may revolutionize evolution on this planet. What can you say about this?

The quantum field too is best understood as the zero state, or nothing, for you can get into the idea that all is born from this one something. It is not so - it is a resting point at which all is ready to go again and again. Not for reason, for this wave does not have purpose - it expands and interacts and changes form and no form. It is born and it does but is never not there for even when the heart stops beating there is a flatline, a resting point is there not? It is a waving, a peak and trough, a high and a low, around and about, and all this time a dance of polarities is really just the dance of one. Do you see this?

8. Is then the quantum field different from the 'ABE' zero-state? Our science says that all energy is contained in this quantum state. Yet it is also at rest. Could you clarify more on what we call the 'quantum'?

No, it is not. For if all is one, how can it be so. It is where you say it is resting point - it is where form is called one. You could liken it to the state of drawing things out of a blind bag, like you are pulling something out of thin air, but this is not true for there is never space and as you evolve you will see this more and more. For you never just pull something from thin air but from an all-inclusive pool of consciousness. Call it quantum, call it ABE, call it you - for all of these answers will be correct. ABE.

9. The known universe is said to be held together by dark energy, and yet our sciences known very little about this. Could you explain dark energy and its significance?

It is a term we like to call a place at which things cannot be measured for this is the zero state; and although we say about the quantum field this is but too the same thing. It is not different; it has a term for science have been able to call it something for it is the point or cusp of creation. Now see this, a tube that can stretch out, circle around back upon itself, all but the same one tube but points of just the same thing - the tube. Is this of understanding?

10. Are you saying that dark energy, zero-state, and ABE are all the same thing – the same state?

Yes. For what is in darkness is just but that which has not seen the light - that being of perception, of the interaction, the splitting apart. Is this of understanding?

11. What are the functions of black holes?

Black holes are just points of different vibratory connections. See this, like the workings of the brain it is necessary for your brain to evolve to make certain neural pathways, connections. This is but so the same for black holes. Is this understood?

12. Could you explain a little more about how black holes function in the cosmos?

Black holes are but the connectors, the points at which when vibrationally aligned will open to reveal a connection, a joining up. See, these pathways are being created within so will then be created without too, to reveal more when the vibrational alignment is connected. When points are joined up, like within the brain, you create a different perception - do you not? Well, this is so for black holes - same thing but outside of yourselves. See, in the resonation you open up more, creating more pathways, until it all just comes back to one. Is this of understanding?

13. The galactic core is said to be an 'engine of energy' – how does this energy affect cosmic evolution?

The galactic core is but the inside of the outside. It is but the centre, but also the very outer. It is not really an effect on cosmic evolution but a part of it. You see, in this world of polarity you have to see a grinder and engine room but is not so. It could very well be a large attraction point like, but you see all is attraction, inter-relational. It is things even beyond this that are keeping it in point of attraction. Your science looks on expandment and should rather be looking at vibration, which is in essence nothing, but understand this you are then of understanding of all and the interrelationship of things. We would like to say one thing that these too are gateways - not for other places but for larger and larger connections vibrationally to be made; a piecing together if you will. ABE.

14. Much has been said about the 'galactic alignment' – is this an important phenomenon and how would it affect processes on this planet?

Yes - you see, the pathways are being carved out; they are of a vibrational essence. All the points are there to make these connections. We say but one thing and it is this - a web of consciousness infinitely expanding. Is this of understanding?

15. Do certain galactic/cosmic alignments have an effect on human consciousness? Do such alignments form a part of the process of planetary evolution?

It is so, for it creates a shift; and in that shift you then create a shift and then back and forth and around and around. You see, it is all communicating vibrationally, and always has. You see, there is a conversation that has been going on - all you have to do is allow and listen. ABE.

16. The scientist-inventor Nikola Tesla knew about the energies of vibration. Was he accessing the unified field? Could you comment upon the work of Nikola Tesla?

He was but a person that was open, that could understand particularly vibration - although has been recently more understood - and was taking this infinite power that everyone is capable of. You see, the people who seem to be ahead of their times are usually seen as crazy for they have allowed this energy to flow forth and in this made the necessary connections. They have evolved, you see, in allowing this you enable it and when you enable it you allow it to manifest in physical form. You are making a necessary connection, and in this evolving. But you must see that this connection is but never lost; it's just that you are on but a different frequency. You are blocking it out; you are of material frequency and life wants to cause you to allow cosmic frequency. Is this of a sufficient answer to this?

17. You said that 'life wants to cause you to allow cosmic frequency' – is this then how we develop and evolve, by allowing cosmic frequency to manifest through us and upon the planet?

It is so. But hear this, you are but never apart from it. You are but blocking it out and shutting it down for you do not understand that part of yourselves; and some who do, have over-conceptualised and tied down something that so just wants to flow. You see, you can still be you – 'you' just have to rhythm up, get in tune, by stopping and listening. ABE.

18. To clarify on the functioning of black holes - you said that they operate like inside of a brain, as if creating new neural pathways. Would black holes be like cosmic synapses, creating pathways to stars and aligning with them vibrationally and energetically?

This is exactly so: like one giant brain, one giant consciousness - all but one thing making its way back to this. ABE.

19. There are many irregularities concerning Earth's moon. Some theories speculate that our planet's moon is an artificial structure. Also, that there are other artificial moons/structures in our solar system. Could you comment on this?

Good morning. Ah, the moon as an artificial structure. If we are completely honest, and we want this communication to always be so, then we would say it is nonsense. There will always be theories, for words are just thoughts and everyone is entitled to their own view. But see here, the world was flat until you found the necessary items to connect up and communicate and interact better with your world, and in this discovering yourselves. For it is always inter-relational and you can only discover and connect the points when the two points are at resonation to one another and vibration is the key to creating these cosmic neural pathways - as within, so without. ABE.

20. Although humans reportedly landed on the moon in 1969, there has been no further manned exploration of the solar system. Could you comment on this?

As we said above, the points of connection have to resonate. But see that they are really not apart at all; it is only apart because of the dissonance between them. It is not because you are separated at all; it is that there is a clouding - a mist, a fog, an engaged line or fault on the line would be a better term - that does not enable you to connect and receive. We keep going back to this. But the brain, as you get older and experience more through life, new pathways are created. This is the same with cosmic pathways - the more you allow the more you see. It is always equal in resonance, and discovering your vibratory essence is key to this shift in consciousness which in turn will create more pathways. It is so tightly interwoven. Is this of understanding? We would like to add that there has not been more exploration for you are shifting as a species and maybe just maybe it is time to discover yourselves fully before you could and would be able to create new pathways. ABE.

21. There has been talk recently of attempting to colonize Mars. Is this a positive – or necessary - move forward for our species evolution? Is our species ready to move off Earth?

We do not feel that it is time to do this yet. As we say, we would see it be for this to benefit the cosmos at all you would really as a whole species have connected more - united within and without. For you see, if you are to do this at present then are you not just bringing more dissonance? We do not feel it is the right time, for you need to discover all that you are and piece it back together. For if as a species you are wanting this colonization from a splintered mind then this will not enable you to move forward. This step, we feel, should always come from a place of unification for it to be of any use or benefit to your species. Love and Light – ABE. We would like to add that just like the brain, the pathways, the connections have to be clear. In this, meaning vibratory flow within is of utmost importance. Is this of understanding?

22. Yes, it makes sense that a species should not consider further colonization in the cosmos until it is unified within. Is this the same understanding with other intelligent species in the cosmos? There is speculation here that other cosmic species may wish to do us harm - that is, they are in dissonance and not in harmony or unity. Could you comment?

It is not the other species at all, not the ones that are further along evolved, for they could of only evolve by seeing this unification. For in the seeing of this is the way you move forward, you evolve. We would be more inclined to say that a species that is splintered would do far more harm. ABE.

23. In terms of species evolution, there can only be a continued development when there is a recognition of unification and a unified mind. Any species which would wish to cause dissonance would be less evolved. Is this correct?

Yes, this is so. But you see, if your very planet is but evolving too then you will have to shift, or you will not be of resonance. This meaning you have to take the jump at some point from a crumbling tower. ABE.

24. You talk about new 'cosmic pathways' opening up as we make the resonating connections. Is this a way of saying that the cosmos - or further 'unknowns' - will make themselves available to us when we show, as a species, that we are ready? If you like, we could say that we create our own quarantine until we can prove we are ready to move out?

You will always create tighter and tighter restrictions when you are of dissonance, of resistance - it is always so. You create your own little boxes through fear of loss of control, but this needs to be loosened now. You as a species have to see this unification, firstly piecing yourself back together - taking back what society has told you and the way in which you have been conditioned. In turn, this will allow you to allow new connections. Your circles will get larger and expansion will come naturally. But it will only ever be from this place of unification. Why make your life harder by forcing pathways when by allowing would be not only easier but more harmonious? ABE.

25. You stated before that the human body will merge with technology that will result in longer life spans. This issue of the human-cyborg is very controversial. Is this biology-technology merger a natural flow in the evolutionary process? Can you talk more on this?

It will be a natural flow and would be beneficial if it is coming from these unforced pathways of evolutionary connection. We are not asking you to sit around and wait. But firstly, know all that you are for if you can really grasp this as a whole species it will surely be a quantum leap for you in evolutionary terms. ABE.

26. Human scientists are experimenting more with biotechnology, such as DNA modification and gene sequencing. There is the probability here of modifying the human body. This is controversial for many people. Is this an inevitable part of our species evolution?

We would like to say too that if, and always, it is coming from a place of unification. For the splintered human is just that – splintered. For if you only had part of the ingredients to make a cake it would not work, it would not be complete; and in this would it even be a cake? You see, there is great intention of making the cake but if you do not have the complete ingredients to make it then you may well end up with something that was not intentional at all. Is this of understanding? The grounding - the unified human - is one to carve greatness into the world; especially into a world that is so splintered. But there is great hope, for all across the planet unification is appearing even in the darkest corners. ABE.

27. Technology is advancing at a rapid pace. We are at a crossroads of where biological life is merging with technology. Some people are calling this a new 'post-human' era. Is it a normal evolutionary drive to replace carbon-based life-forms with technology-machine intelligence? What can you say about this?

It is not, no. More so, we would like to say as to support the biological functioning if need be. But we see that the way in which you are going is not from a place of unification - of knowing of this vibrational essence to everything. You really cannot delay this any longer for your species is on the cusp of moving forward. This is why we have continued to manifest, to say 'hold on – let's get this part right first and then when we truly understand this, then we can move forward.' We are not saying that you should listen to us at all but listen and feel to yourselves. Understand yourselves first and foremost before you take a step forward - from a place of love and understanding and not from a place as to which to be a winner of the race. ABE.

28. We agree that our species evolution should not be a race or competition. Yet it seems as if there is another race between the evolution of our awareness about our unitary essence and technological development. If our awareness does not advance sufficiently, doesn't this indicate for problematic futures?

They can only do so if you are not wise, if you are asleep to it. If you don't play the game, then there is no game to play - is it not true? You see, it will cause dissonance for if there is dissonance within then surely it be shown in your very existence and in all you do. Harmonize within and see that this will shine out. You see, when you have a light it cancels out the darkness. It does not eradicate it, but light is shone upon what was only once unseen. We are not saying you should be a perfect species, for there is no such ideal, but to know truly and understand truly without a doubt that in which you are. It is not so to say all should listen and lord this information over each and every one of you. No, but to awaken that little spark to nudge the heart as if to say, 'life is here, it is waiting.' That is all we can ever wish to do. The rest is really up to yourselves. ABE.

We would also like to say that this should never be preached or say that we are right, that this is truth. But to allow you to feel these words in the center of your very being for you to know that what we speak of as truth.

29. Have there been other planets that passed through an advanced technological evolution? If so, how did they experience this process?

There is, and there have – yes. Every planet is differing in its needs of these differing technological advancements. But see this, it is all to be used and only to enhance the organism. So be very wary if your species is using these in ways to control and manipulate, for they are not the purpose for someone who is coming from a place of unification at all. We have seen this battle before, but it can be overcome by knowing that in which you are - knowing your power and place of resonance. Controlling and manipulation will always try to push forth. In some sense, it is in the knowing of what you are is where your power really lies. ABE.

30. There are international efforts to develop forms of artificial intelligence. This could be incredibly positive for the evolution of human civilization or highly problematic. What can you say about artificial intelligence?

Again, we feel like a stuck record; but this is only truth. It needs to be from this place of unification always. We see that there are people in power and who have the money and resources to do this now who one could say is not of unification and are very much in it for the race. But you see, you always think that you are powered by such people when in reality it is the other way around. The masses are awakening to this dissonance - they are claiming back their power. Artificial intelligence will be of benefit if, like we say, it is a tool, an enhancement to the lives of others. Otherwise, it is of no use for it will be in the wrong hands. ABE.

We are by no means saying that this transition to unification will be a complete easy ride, for there will be destruction and dismantling of old structures. But see this, it is making way for these new connections that have unified within and therefore can only unify without, claiming back your evolutionary stance. ABE.

31. With increased automation of our lives more and more people will be compelled to find answers for the role and function of the human being. How can people seek for meaning in an increasingly controlled world?

Meaning is always that in which you make it, always. It is never outside of you. You have been conditioned in such a way that this is always sought outside of yourselves, but it is not so. One can find meaning in the seemingly mundane where others it is doing great. What we would like to say that all meaning is, is really just connection. Like the universe wants to know itself through itself, so this is true for you. Connect, be open, be true. ABE.

32. Powerful technologies – such as cyber and bio-technologies – are increasingly in the hands of small groups or even individuals. Will this create a dissonance of power relations that could create greater uncertainty amongst humanity?

If people are wise to what they are; if they stand strong in the knowing of this unification, then they would not even entertain the game at all. It is only when you are splintered that you are powerless. There will be a struggle of power between people claiming theirs back and the few who remain to want to manipulate and control. And they will do so through fear, but the harmonization of such will balance out. We are never claiming of what your species see as all good - this is a world of polarity. But bringing back to balance is key - centering yourselves first. ABE.

33. Virtual/Augmented reality and video games are increasingly popular amongst the young people. These interactions also have the capacity to re-wire our brains, do they not? Some people are worried about young people's fixation with such activities. Could you comment on this?

Yes, it does but re-wire and re-adjust. It is about balance. But see this, they are of understanding that this is so a game - for the ones that are of entrapment are really the ones stuck in a reality and are unaware that they are but playing a game at all. Is this of understanding?

34. What advice could you give us about the development and use of technologies?

The only advice we would like to give is use them to enhance life and be very wary if a technological advancement creates dissonance rather than connection, for this will only be moving you away further from the truth, enabling the few to keep this power and redeeming you as powerless. All technological advancement, if more and more become unified, will enable you to explore yourselves, your world, and the cosmos more. And in this waking up, more and more people creating greater and greater neural pathways within and without in the cosmos. This will, of course, need your species to evolve, to advance in some way. But always it should be of promoting connection and pathways. ABE.

We would also like to add, if you are prompting us to state what technological advancements will occur, then we would like to say that we are understanding that technology is advancing at a rapid pace and it seems to be very much still in the hands of the few who may use such technologies to create dissonance. More so, what we have to say is that it will only be balanced out again or taken back if people are wise to it - not everyone, for like a wave it will spread anyway. But for these new pathways to be formed there has to be that first step - that first one or few who will walk it first and say, 'look, it is not so scary as you think.' Do you understand why we talk so much about getting this key foundation set first? We leave you now with much love and light and great gratitude to be able to come forth. ABE.

35. Life extension is now a major research area. Some scientists wish to eradicate death. This sounds good, but is it wise to try to eliminate the natural dying of our bodies? This could be problematic for vibrational signatures as well as over-population. Could you comment on this?

It will always be of your sciences and technological establishments that want to eradicate the natural processes of life. And although it is seen as a good thing to prolong life, we do so feel it should be more of a natural process. But hear this, we are not at all discounting your advancement as a species, and although life expectancy will be prolonged due to technological advancements and the morphing of biological and technical, we do so feel that in a biological sense it should still be of a natural process. It is also so that you are changing in form with these new vibrations, so there will also be a natural evolutionary process to your being. But as we see it, you cannot rush this process too far forward. Of course, you can push the boundaries of life, but what we want to say is that it must always take in this whole picture. Now, we understand that you would very much like to prolong your experience in physical form. But we also see the need not to meddle in it too much, for you will upset the natural rhythm if pushed too far and that could be catastrophic. For not only you but to that of the whole cosmos. You see that there is a fine line between enhancing and completely dominating, controlling, and forcing life for all life is a balancing act and really you must see this place of unification as we see it. To advance much more balanced, much more smarter and much more in flow, trying not to cause further dissonance. ABE.

36. Following on from the above, there was a news report released today stating that birth rates had radically fallen in the last half a century. Perhaps natural processes will adjust for such things as population and we don't need to try to overtly socially manage this?

It is true that you do need to take a step back at some point to allow balance to appear. Now see this, balance can look destructive and chaotic like things are far from balance for your social constructs have built their buildings upon changeable foundations. You see that you as humans in your own lives, for example, you do not know when things will change and take a different course. You see life has this funny way of changing direction within a heartbeat - come back to yourself, feel back into your bodies. Bring all those vibrational attachments back in and just see even if for just a moment in this deep rest. Even if just momentarily, you will have a deep sense of the world and your part within it. You will see that there is a time for doing and there is a time to sit and just watch the grass grow. ABE.

37. Time, as we measure it, is a linear path, based on solar movement and planetary effects. Understandably, time as we experience it is a local phenomenon. Yet there is also much speculation on the science of time-travel. Could you say something about how 'time' is experienced or recognized throughout the cosmos?

It is very much of linear process, yes, in your physical existence. For in a sense, it is in harmony for you at this stage in time in your evolutionary process. You see time as around and around on your clocks, but as a line of points at to which can be recorded too. Now, which one could it be? That time is of a circular pattern re- repeating itself, or could it be a long line in which things appear upon and are recorded and dated? But you come to know that time is only but a social construct; to say, I was here and I can prove it because, you see, I existed from one time to another. It was really a mere measurement of existence of individual things at differing times. Now, what we say is if you took away your clocks and your timelines for a mere moment you would see that it is only here, now. And although we do not like the concept of 'now,' for it has been over-used, it is but a statement of continuous becoming, and you are never apart from it. The functionings of your vibrational signature allow you to ponder upon the future by thinking about the past. But you see, you are here with it - there is nowhere to get to so long as you can see that and not be attached to future or longing for past. That you are merely here with life and able to do these wondrous things within this time-space reality. You see, we are never here to say 'be here' for it is a wondrous gift to be able to think of the future and mull over past experience - that is being human and being of physical form. It is the attachment to race ahead or drag yourselves back to what once was. You see that there is no time, just a becoming and to state that there is a now and you should be in it is also a false premise, a past - for the moment you try to become present it has already passed, has it not? Throughout the whole of the cosmos you experience time differently. Some, no time at all; just an interaction of being. And some that have made these new pathways through evolutionary process and vibrational connection to allow them to jump time – time, in regards to your measurement - of the one thing, the one happening, the one constant and infinite becoming. ABE.

38. As we shift into a new phase of human civilization we will require new forms of energy extraction and distribution. Scientists are working hard on nuclear fusion/fission, hydrogen power, and similar forms that use atomic elements. Yet is there a way to utilize the quantum or zero energy to provide for our needs? Isn't it time that we understood how to access new energy forms that are cosmic rather than planetary?

It is, and you will step into this process only when you are of full understanding of vibration and unification. There is infinite power in this source of zero state. But you see, you can harness this for yourselves for this too is of you and from the world around. No longer will you have to rely upon physical material sources to power your world, but to look to vibrational attraction for this is the key that holds much power. But hear this, you must also firstly - and this is of great importance - come to this place of unification for this power could be used for destruction rather than benefiting yourselves as a species. Is this of understanding now?

39.Are we likely to discover and utilize a science of vibrations within this century? Where will science go from here? What can we expect next?

Science is moving forward, and they are becoming more and more so aware of the unseen and even the unmeasurable. But hear this, they have not yet fully unified this, for they are still very much separate things. When science can see the vibrational element is really no differing from that of your physical existence it will go much further. It will make these pathways, these neural pathways, clear to join up. If they could firstly join up matter and vibration, well, science will excel and in this will cause you to join up the dots within. We cannot say a specific time for it is all about the allowance of this connection which is trying to pave a new path. We see that it will be of great significance over the next 10 years or so in the discovery of moving forward to a more unified existence, and in this an emergence of one could say spirit and matter. But hear this, when science knows undoubtedly that these two things were never of separation at all - that there was merely a fault on the line, a contamination of sorts – well, it will be of fast movement forwards. Of infinite expansion of mind, a more cosmic communicative system. For you see, in the move forward your brain expands; it creates new pathways and in this you create this within the cosmos too. And with this you become more of a communicative race without the need of material substance. Is this of understanding?

40. Some popular scientists are publishing books about how to create colonies on other planets and interstellar travel, etc. They say this is the future of humanity. Are they preparing the human species in advance? Or is this misconceived belief and a result of the splintered mind?

We would like to say it is of advancement, but we see so much that there is very much still this splintered mind. See this, an allowance of vibration to a splintered mind, the flow, is there - it can never not be. But it is but falling upon an object that will split apart and not fully understand this unification. Now, if you were to allow and also understand unification it will flow through the process. You would be the channel that brings connections rather than the one that allows, and then sifts, and sorts, and places through your own vibrational signature. And although we always say that it is not to be rid of it, is in the knowing of when to put it aside and to be of service to yourself, and in this to the whole. Is this of understanding?

41. Our science still believes that space travel will be accomplished by forms of energy propulsion. Is it not more probable that humanity will explore the cosmos through extended consciousness rather than physical bodies?

We do so see this, yes, for now. But it will be of sorts to come that you will not need apparatus to visit, for your bodies will be differing. See it like this, you hear of near-death experiences to be that some see God or enter heaven and see loved ones. This is but the vibrational signature not leaving the body. For we do not see start and end, or that of a soul. This is why we use vibrational signature for it is what one would call mind too. They have these experiences for even though the body is dead the consciousness is not so. The vibrational signature is back into the zero state although never being apart - it just does not have the channel in which to express through. It is into this cosmic consciousness, if you will, just a different state. The reason that people can remember this and although being clinically dead in your material existence, there is a point in which vibrational alignment or resonance is still to that of this body and its conditionings. We understand that this may of gone off of the question quite a bit, but what we are really trying to express is that the more pathways that are created through you, and then within the cosmos, the less need there will be to explore in a physical sense for you will see that consciousness is but free to travel and is not as constrained as you once thought so. ABE.

42. The advancement of computation has given us the perspective that the cosmos operates similar to a kind of program. Some people speculate that we are living inside of a grand cosmic computer program and that our lives are like a simulation. Would this be a suitable analogy?

We would rather but see it more so as an evolutionary process, more so a brain. You see, we talk about these neural pathways and we mean that for both on the material level and also that of the cosmos level. Is this of understanding? For you see, if there is just one thing and you are it, then what is within is also without on a larger scale - a going back if you will to the Russian doll analogy. ABE.

43. Many people now experience synchronicities in their lives, and 'signs' as if - they say - the 'universe' is speaking to them. Are there such interventions where messages are placed into the material realm?

Not so much a placement but of an allowance. But you see, you have to be aware of them too. But hear this, some people get so caught up in the signs and synchronicities they grab a hold of them - as in a way to know and therefore control or resist certain experience. You see, there is always a knowing of sorts if you are allowing; and allowing is knowing. And then in this the universe is then always in communication with you. ABE.

44. New technologies are likely to be more accessible to the elites - especially such things as genetic enhancement. Isn't there a possibility that the human race will be divided by this rather than unified?

It is so a possibility. But you see, are you not then putting continued power to those at the top so to speak? You see, they are interested in power and at present power is money. This will shift course, and of course there will be someone who will want to manipulate whatever commodity is of utmost importance for your survival as a species. You will see that in the shifting of yourselves there will be a shifting of power. It will be placed back into the hands of the many rather than the few. But hear this, it will be a struggle for you have allowed it for such a long time and have left many things dormant and gathering dust. It is not a battle of power as such; more so, a shift. Is this of understanding? We would also like to add that a unified being is of utmost importance now for this is where you will gain all your power back - all your pieces that have been splintered for so long. Yes, there will be technological advancements and no doubt be people that will want to control and manipulate. With this we are not stating a euphoric existence but a real one. But you see, the more and more people that are understanding and knowing of this unification, this vibration in which you are being shifted to resonate with, to understand, the more these structures will not be able to withhold. For you see, the animals that became extinct were the ones that could not resonate to their systems; and therefore, could not continue into the new vibrational evolution. Is this of understanding now?

45. To bring back power to the masses, we need to shift our vibrationary state – to drop our social conditionings, our ego, our fixed identities, and to allow a connection for consciousness to flow. If people can resonate to a new state of being, then so will our social systems shift and evolve. Is this what you are saying?

Yes, this is true. But see, these things do not have to be dropped permanently and cannot. One could liken it to a good clear-out of such, then put back once you have given the shelving a good dusting. Is this of understanding?

46. It seems obvious that technology is now a permanent part of our human lives. At the same time there will be a need to be closer to Nature - maybe a wish to return to more agrarian lifestyles. How can this seeming contradiction between high technology and pastoral living be balanced?

It can be used to harness this zero-state - this vibrational attraction - for it can power your life in such a way that there will be no need to rip apart your world to create more power. It will also be in such a way that your own being is the power point and there will be no need for others to control and manipulate. For how could one manipulate if all you need is all you have right now? In this it will create more of a unified field of communication, not only in your physical existence but that of the cosmos too. ABE.

47. Scientists have constructed a complex particle accelerator – the Hadron collider – to search for new particles and to examine unsolved questions in physics. Some people view these experiments as risky. Is this a wise way to operate in order to know the cosmos better?

You see, there will always be things that come up for you to scrutinize and pinpoint a point of your existence. It is done so in a way to utilize power; to create points at which this power can be utilized. Which way that seems to go is unclear. For as we like to say, a splintered mind/ being is far more likely to use this for their own gains rather than using it for a more unified purpose. We see that scientists are getting the focus to smaller and smaller particles to enable them to figure out your material existence. But see this, the more and more focused it becomes the more it is pinpointed, the more splintered your existence becomes. Open up and you will see the greatest power source and in this you will discover yourselves. We are not saying that you should not become focused on the details but firstly you need to open up, then to re-adjust. ABE.

48. Scientists note that our local galaxy – which we call the Milky Way – contains around a billion planets that are 'Earthlike' in their properties. Our strongest telescope can spot about 100 million galaxies in the visible universe. In an earlier communication you stated that there are only 5 planets in the cosmos, including ours, that is at an advanced stage of evolution. Isn't this a small number compared to the potentials?

It is. But see this, there are more that harbor life in a different way. What we are saying is that there is only a small amount that are in relation to your type of physicality of being. This is not to mean that you are a minority. Far from that, but a small part of differing life spread across all of the cosmos. You see, it is only now as technology has evolved that you are discovering what has been in your deepest oceans for millennia. Is this of understanding?

49. Contact with other advanced intelligences, say our scientists, is more likely to come from powerful electronic brains rather than humanoid, biological species. How close is this to the truth?

We would like to say that it is not so, for you always have that in which you need. See this, you are always receiving; you are never apart from this. It is only in your vibrational signature that is contaminating connection in a way. But you see, it would not serve you either to be rid of it. It is always about the whole, the unification of things. If you can really get to grips with this, then there will be no limits. But you see, you have been contaminated with the notion that you are a physical being and even though this is so there is much more to you than that. It is in the resonance of allowing your being to accept and allow new forms, new pathways, new ways of communication. If you do not understand this unification, then it will not serve you to open up; for it will cause dissonance of vibrations in which you hold. Is this of understanding?

50. How can we build up, or develop, our means on communication with the cosmos and other non-terrestrial intelligences?

Trust in what you are, knowing of this unified system, allowing vibrational resonance, allowing open heart communication. But see this, before you are to try this be sure for it to be firmly rooted into your being, into all that you do on this level first. ABE.

51. Science sees physical evolution on the earth as related to environmental factors, including phases of glaciation. But are not phases of consciousness 'directed' and managed as evolutionary impulses upon the earth?

You see, the Earth evolves in physicality and then the species upon that planet have no choice but to move with it. You see, your planet is evolving, and you are doing so in unison. See it like this, you are at a place of work and they put in a new technological advancement to help be more productive. They get rid of the old system and install a new one. Now the workers will have to adapt, will have to learn new ways of being. If not, they could be let go of for they will not be beneficial to the whole operation. Is this of understanding? We are not trying to denounce your part as human beings for it is a true gift. But we are merely trying to put forth that when your planet shifts you have no other choice but to shift with it and this goes further and further out until zero state again, and back around and re-creating and changing form and no form. It is so tightly intertwined but always at the core is pure consciousness, just reflecting and retracting and shifting and dancing. Is this of understanding?

52. Are you saying that past human species went extinct because they were unable to adjust to the earth's evolving shifts and resonance?

Yes, this is what we are but saying. For something to grow - and this is such for you as individuals - some things have to be dropped, they cannot go forward on the same paths. Like the seed that wanted to grow so much, it bust apart all that it was and in this had taken on another form. Is this of understanding?

53. Technology is often regarded as referring to mechanical-type devices. Is there not also a 'spiritual technology' whereby we can develop our internal senses. Perhaps even re-wire our brains and nervous system? What would you say about this?

For is not technological, or as you state mechanical type devices, still but an expression of this, of this one thing? For it has come through but the physical organism through consciousness. What makes the complete difference between them is what vibration it is being filtered through - splintered or unified?

54. The science of intention and manifestation is both recognized and yet similarly ignored by many. How is internal intention related to external manifestation in our reality?

It is but a filter of consciousness you can allow what is meant to be for you. For you see, it has been a big thing for so long and has been made such a big fuss of and in this you really have contaminated the line. The pathways have been stopped dead in their tracks. For you have tried to be positive and although it may have its benefits it is very much splintered and much cause of dissonance. We are not saying at all to be passive but unification in oneself is much more a powerful force in the world than a splintered vibration. You can have an intention, you always will for your physical existence. But see this, allow it to come; loosen up the grips of what is meant to be for your very essence knows the path and you have to trust in that. Once more, open up that heart and allow. ABE.

55. We feel that science and technology are focusing too much upon the externals of physical existence, whereby we need now to focus on the intangible, non-physical aspects if we are to successfully develop as a species. Could you comment on this?

It is true, and this is what we mean also in the taking it back to the bare bones. For you are stripping all condition away, which is very much a physical thing, to reach back to this zero-state, and say 'now we're gathering things all back together.' For in this nothing, in this unseen non-physical part of existence, is the key to many leaps forward as a species - and creating new neural pathways within and without. Is this of understanding now?

56. Thank you ABE, for your patience with us. We hope to continue this communication and further allow this understanding. Is there anything else you would wish to communicate before we finish this session?

We are glad to be discussing such things and is well and good to ask these questions for they are of importance and are of depth to communicate well that in which we want to put forth. We do hope that this is to continue, and we see things aligning for next steps to be taken. We wish for you to connect and follow your own guidance for that too is but us and also of you. We would like to say but one thing and that is we really want you to see what a true gift it is to be in physical form and although we try to walk in the middle by neither being overly positive as to delude you of a perfect future, we do not either want to instill fear for this is not our purpose. Our true purpose is to hand it all back - all the constraints that have been put upon you by others and all those that you have put upon yourselves. We hope to continue this communication. ABE.

Chapter Twelve

Humanity & its Future

1. Many people consider humanity to be at a crossroads where a breakthrough or a breakdown is more sensitive. To survive this phase will depend on our state of consciousness and whether we shift quick enough from a splintered to a unified mind? What can you say about this?

Yes, this is but true that evolution is one of conscious unity. See it like this, your consciousness is like the glue that will piece what you really are back together again if you so allowed it. But your vibrational signature but separates and boxes things up. This is due to your social conditioning. You see, it blinkers out this state of being in order to make you a good citizen. Seldom do people allow this into their everyday conscious experience, and in this they have the blinkers on. They do not have the full picture; they do not operate at full capacity and to live a life in such a way - a life that could be so much more - is the greatest shame of your human experience. But see this, you can only have a breakthrough if you have a breakdown of old paradigms; and if old is crumbling then it paves way for new pathways, new connections, and in this breakdown there will be great breakthrough as people will be searching within themselves for something that resonates; something that sticks; something that makes them so feel human again. ABE.

2. What are likely to be the consequences if humanity, as a whole, is unable to recalibrate its balance and resonance with the planet? What timescales are we talking about?

You see, it does not work in such a way for it is in unison - not one to full vibrational capacity, then other; no, but an inter-relational nudging. You see, there is a lot to be said already for vibrational resonance. For people are changing and you can see there is much balance within. The reason for us to come forth is because we see that this resonance is tipping the scales again in a way that people are still engrossed in their own vibrational signatures. For they are understanding this unified field, but they are shifting to make it into something special, something above and beyond, something that you have to aspire to or make yourselves equal to - you have to be better, to not get angry or sad. But you see, this would not be of balance at all and would not be of a human experience. The only way to unity is accepting the light and the dark, the love and the hate, as but the same thing because within this unity you realize that you are perfectly imperfect, and that is wonderful. Is this of understanding? When you ask but of a timescale to this, we would be so inclined to say within the next century. For you see, to really uproot what has been common knowledge, for humanity needs to also be uprooted from the minds of humanity and this will take time for people will feel a gaping hole where what once stood a statue of self, and you had built your whole world around it. But you see, this gap does not need to be filled again but to allow life to flow uninstructed through your being. We would like to strip things back to the name of 'no name' for even after all this communication with us you too will even have to drop us to see this truth also. ABE.

3. We dream about the future. Some people say they can see into the future. Surely the future is a set of potentials rather than a fixed destiny? What can you say about this?

We would be inclined to say that it is but both. Now see this, there are fixed outcomes as an inevitability. For example, you throw an egg at a wall; in its natural state it is going to smash. But there are many differing factors that could be changed in order to give a different outcome if you're consciously aware. Say, for example, you make a target you are more certain as to where that would hit. Or, if you did so boil the egg first it would most probably not smash the egg at all; well, not in the way it would do so as before. Is this of understanding?

4. Humans are dreamers. What happens to our vibrational signature during the sleep state? Do our dreams have significance?

This is but the time that you give up this vibrational signature. You are at resting point and you see you are back to zero state - you are unified. We would rather but see dreaming as waking up for you are so conditioned to be active and doing. We are not saying that this should be such a way for your physical existence, but of unified collaboration, conscious and unconscious - the whole picture. For in this state of being you are allowing and also able to act. You are aware and also allowing - this is resonance of your very being. This is resonance to your planet, and this is resonance to the universe. ABE.

5. Life seems to be so highly complex and yet based upon some very simple laws. What are these laws?

The laws are − − − − for there are no laws. For the moment you speak you have taken it away from that in which it really is. But we see this may not suffice as good for us to give an explanation of how the world or cosmos works. So, we say this - it is all and will always ever be a vibrational resonance. This is true across all times, all space; and when resonance happens, physicality is created. You have long forgotten your vibrational essence and how it is tying and binding itself to things and places and people and experiences, and future outcomes and past problems. One simple thing; one thing – vibration. Remember this and you really do remember yourselves. Bring this into your conscious minds and you will see it in all that you interact with. Is this of understanding?

6. We have been told before by other teachings to 'raise our vibration.' It sounds good. Yet it also sounds abstract and New Age. How can we explain to the average person to raise their vibration?

You allow it. Strip it back; all the conditions in which you have put upon life, upon yourselves, and upon others. Give life room to move again within you, for there isn't a state to get to - it is here. It's just that you have the blinkers on, the social blinkers - take those off and allow all that you are. See the unity in all that you do, and your vibration will be nothing but resonance to your world, to each other. In this you will be creating heart-to-heart connections in all that you do. ABE.

7. If a person begins to shift their vibrational resonance, this will affect others in whom they come into contact with – like a transmitter? Isn't this one aspect of how change can manifest, by positively infecting others, so to speak?

You can do so. But see this, if their vibrational essence is one of pure resistance then it will at first not have any flow. But hear this, it is of not forcing at all but of you continuously resonating at that at which you are - and in this it will break through at some point, weathering away at that contamination. The only thing you can do is not allow it to contaminate yours. If so, it is but a good idea to strengthen your own connection before trying to change that of others. Is this of understanding now?

8. The truth of reality is so difficult for our rational, splintered minds to grasp. We wish to understand that we can access connections with the cosmic mind/unified consciousness, yet it seems so far away from our everyday lives. How can we shift into a state of knowing?

You see, like we said before you have been conditioned in such a way to block it out and to hurry up and just get on with it. For this will make you easy to handle, predictable, and safe - but this is not true. In this conditioning you have become more and more disconnected. For a splintered mind creates just that - a splintered world, and in that a splintered cosmos. To move forward you have to understand that this is how it is. That it is all but a unified field - and we are not bad, we are it. In this realization that we are it, in this deep knowing that 'oh yes, its all the same and I am it too,' you let up the character. It is not so important you let yourselves and others off the hook. But see this, it is a process, it is a becoming. Of this there are lots of conditioning to unwrap. Is this of understanding?

To shift into a state of knowing then, you have to be allowing. Your current paradigm is one of resistance to what is not physical and in this you shut out vibration. You shut out yourselves, tightening the conscious experience, restricting it. The only way to allow is to rest. Just for now, gather in all the wires of intention, the hooks of belief - reel them back in just for now and rest. Gather and recalibrate the system – harmonize, unite.

9. There will be many people who will consider it crazy that a 'unified zero state field' called ABE is speaking to them. What would you say to them?

Ahh, yes. It would be so such a way because you have been conditioned in such a way as to shut this out, for it is not of service, to keep order and obedience. But you see, the name is not of importance at all. For like we said, even after this connection and writings - and there will be but plenty more writings - we would say drop it too, for you are allowing zero state to come forth and in this you are allowing all that you are. You are allowing pure consciousness to express in physical form. This is not available to just the few but to each and every one, if they do so allow. Drop it all and allow. Is this of understanding now?

10. Some may say that the age of religion is over. We no longer need the crutches of intermediary teachings when we can access Source directly. Is humanity moving into an era of conscious communication with Source? Is this necessary to evolve further as a species on this planet?

It is this way, yes. You are but moving into a different pathway, a conscious evolution. It is so that in the loosening of your own individual vibrational signatures you allow more and more of this energy in - this vibration. We do not want you to be rid of your vibrational signature for this will never be so. But you see, in the allowance of the new vibration it shakes loose the contamination that has been considered your vibrational signature for so long. You will harmonize your vibrational signature with that of the zero-state vibrational essence. It will be of resonance, not of riddance. Is this of understanding now?

It is of essence to move forward. But you see, at some point you have to STOP, readjust, and then move forward again from a different place.

11. We've changed our life rhythms. Rather, our new technological environment has altered our rhythms, and we've not had sufficient time biologically, as well as psychologically, to adjust. What would you say about this?

It is true. Technology has created dissonance in such a way that your evolution has been stunted. You see, it has to be that unified nudging, and you have not been inclined to feel that nudge. Now, it has to be more so of a blow rather than a nudge. You see, technological advancement will always serve humanity from its own state of consciousness, and at present it is still very much splintered. To really make it of use you can see from the worldwide web that it is all about connections and widening your communicative scope, your consciousness. Is this of understanding, for you see it is always relational?

We would also like to say but one thing - you see, it is never about ridding life of yourselves: sitting upon a hilltop void of self, void of world, no. But what it is, is to take away the false self that has been socially constructed. Let that go, allow this vibrational essence to flow through your being, birthing a new vibrational signature - a non-splintered one, a unified one. It is almost like taking off the band-aid on a cut, allowing the body to harmonize and heal. This is what we come forth; for not to have no self - although there really is no self - but to allow a more harmonized self. The birthing of a whole new humanity, one consciousness at a time, one vibrational alignment at a time. We are grateful for this communication and will continue as long as need be. ABE.

12. Thank you, ABE. What you say sounds similar to what was said by the Indian mystic Aurobindo. He referred to the 'Supramental' or 'Overmind' and how we need to allow it to manifest through us - to 'bring in' this unified consciousness. What can you say about this?

It is so. A collaboration, as you would say, in your physical existence of minds. But mind is vibrational signature and vibrational signature is caused by the vibrational resonance, to create pathways within the brain. This is exactly what it is like outside of you - like a web of consciousness within it so now needs to be allowed without also. Is this of understanding?

13. So, are you saying that one of the functions of the human being is to collaborate with the unified consciousness, to develop resonance, and allow pathways for a pure consciousness to manifest? That is, to form more pathways of connection and unity?

Yes, it is. It is about widening your field of consciousness - opening up the dolls of being contained within another and another until you see 'but oh yes, I am that and that is but me, I were just encased.' Is this of understanding?

14. Humanity is mapping the world and the cosmos like never before. We are seeking deep into the oceans. We are mapping the entire solar system, and our telescopes search deep into the cosmos. What will we find if we don't first find ourselves?

Nothing. You can only ever but find yourselves. But if so coming from a splintered mind, you are finding everything else but yourselves. Is this of understanding?

15. Many people - from scientists to philosophers – are saying that we are entering a post-human era. How can we be going 'post' human if we haven't yet discovered what being human truly means?

This is why it is of utmost importance to strip it back, figure out this part of yourselves in which has been closed off. In the realization of yourselves you see all that you are and all that you have ever been, and that is the whole thing. And from this point new pathways will be open, new things will be seen, new resonance. But see this, they will be new to the eyes that have not yet been open but old news to those that have been awake. ABE.

16. It can be said that the human is both 'being and becoming' – this seems to suggest a combination between a state of rest and a state of evolving. Is there some truth to this?

Yes. It is always this so - you have to be in tune with what you are to allow these subtle shifts to take course within you and create new horizons outside of you.

17. Can you give some examples when the pure consciousness was manifested upon our planet?

It is always a flow, but I realize you are asking who or what has brought it forth before and we can say that there has been many, and this has always been in relation to that of the pathways that are so created at the time of being. It is really manifested in all that you do. But see this, it is but always dependent upon the pathways within the vibrational signature of how this manifests in your world. This is why we are coming forth - to allow a recalibration, a reset if you will. To harmonize what is available to you at your next evolutionary step of creating vibrational pathways - not only within but without too. Is this of understanding?

18. By recalibrating our resonance and alignment, are we also physically re-wiring connections in our brain? Is this what is meant by our potential for neuro-plasticity?

It is so, yes. You are not only doing so with the brain but also DNA is receiving this new shift, this new alignment. All is in conversation - it just depends upon what conversation it is, and what you are so to allow. ABE.

19. Would this mean that old patterns or neural connections will become obsolete because they are no longer of resonance? If this is so, then this would also cause habit patterns in our lives to be broken down too, wouldn't it?

Yes, this is so. Connections will be lost within and this will also affect your outer lives too. This may look like loss, but it is only opening up for new pathways to be formed which are more of resonation to your being and to that of which is trying to manifest in form. ABE.

20. You have spoken much about humanity's splintered mind. What other things do we need to change or shift in order to better harmonize with our future?

Firstly, this unification of self - that is it. We do not want to give but a long 'to do' list. Just this for now - find this. ABE.

21. The future is a complex subject. We understand you may not wish to disclose too much – yet what can you tell us about humanity's future?

It is always in but relation to that of which you have unified. For the path, for so long, has been one of restriction of consciousness. You are on the other side of becoming a round-about circle, and when but this phase has come once you have readjusted, reset. You are but setback on becoming. Take, for example, a child riding a bike - you gently direct and readjust for the child can take this or leave it. It is completely up to them and in this it creates the paths. Is this of understanding?

You see, it is very simple; and by labelling and scrutinizing something you then loose the very meaning. It is to be seen, to be watched, to be felt - for in this the secrets of the universe are revealed. And in this you realize that there was never a secret to be found - you just had to allow yourself to fall back into resonance into you. Is this of understanding?

22. You have mentioned about becoming harmonized to what is available to us at our next evolutionary step. Could you explain more what you mean by this?

Yes, but of course. You see, it is really about allowing - like the wave that has a high and a low, a rest and peak. It could be likened of action and inaction; this is allowing resonance. Knowing but when to rest and see, and readjust, before taking off into action. This is but the lower point of the vibrational wave, and to fuss and fight and to have to constantly keep it in a straight line of resonance you are in hindsight flat-lining life. It is a constant balance between the two, and to know when is where you have to re-attune yourselves. Is this of understanding?

You see, there are many belief systems and constructs that tell you to pick a side and stick with it, and life does not move in such a way. Life is a wave of vibrational potential.

23. Following on from what you say about the high and low points of vibrational waves. Does this suggest that currently humanity is at a 'lower point' on the vibrationary wave? That higher energies are coming that will shift this trajectory?

It is to say that. But do not take higher and lower as, to say, in your own constructs, sense of the words, for they are of equal resonance. But yes, you are but in a dip. It is the time to readjust, realign, and then move forth. For if not so, you will continue with this path of resistance and constant action. Is this of understanding?

You see, in the constant path of action you are but killing life. You are straightening it out, and also it goes for the other end of constant rest. It has to be of resonance - of movement, of rest, of breath. ABE.

That energy is always there; it is just that the evolution is one of consciousness now. It always, but always, has to be in resonance to the mechanism or organism that is receiving such vibrations. Is this of understanding?

24. What is the source for this 'dip' in vibrational resonance - is it due to cosmic conditions? Is it that the organism (humanity) has not evolved in line to receive the vibrations of consciousness - are we in need of a nudge?

It is such this. But also, just local. For like we say, there are at this point contained vibrational waves and dips which are of locality - physical points like the synapses. You see, the vibrational essence or resonance that would connect the two have to be of resonance. The connections cannot and will not be made until your own individual pathways have been readjusted, reset, and reunited. Is this of understanding now?

We are but the nudge. But you are also of that too. ABE.

25. So, until this readjustment and realignment can occur, humanity is, in a sense, 'cut off' from the full cosmic connection and communication. As a species, we need to develop our collective synapse in order to create the pathway, the bridge. Is this a fair description?

It is, yes. At some point you need to stop - gather and rest, readjust, and realign with this wave, this vibration. It is like when you sing too fast in a song and get ahead of yourselves or are too slow and therefore you are still far behind. It is of a mutual emergence. Is this of understanding?

A mirror, a dance of vibrational resonance. ABE.

26. And this readjustment can begin with individuals? Does it require a 'tipping point' - a sufficient mass - rather than a whole species adjustment?

It has to be started there from the beginning. Like we say, back to the barebones of things. For there is but too much noise, too much contamination. Of course, it will always be so - that the more weight in the scale will tip the balance just that tiny bit. What we want to say, that indeed it does not have to be the whole species but a balance of sorts. Is this of understanding?

You see, it will be this way and more and more will follow. Like the cycle we talk of, you're stepping into a dip, whereas the old action orientated resonance is too much - it is going around again to rebalance. But see this, it will always be a kind of tug-of-war to keep balance. For you see, when someone likes a certain food they would want more and more, and in this get tired of it at some point. It will not resonate, so it will go back to zero and rethink about the choices. This can be likened to that of this kind of scenario. Is this of resonance to you? Can you see that in which we speak? For it is always a becoming. ABE.

27. How do you sense this will unfold? Personally, we have a positive view on humanity's future. How does ABE consider the readjustment process, or period?

It will be one of discomfort, for all readjustment is uncomfortable. For if you have been sitting in a certain position for a while when you come to move to another position it is of discomfort, is it not? But this discomfort remains to be seen as to how tightly you hold on to outdated paradigms and how allowing you are to this vibration. That's why you see it is a time to stop and see. Is this of understanding?

28. Will this discomfort period cover the rest of what we call the 21st century? Or will it be a shorter span? (We realize it is somewhat difficult to talk about time lengths).

You see, this that it is so. But if you are able to tip the balance just a little, we would see this be happening within the next 10 years. But see this, it will be a tug-of-war between what is and what wants to become. And could even see this time shortened, so long as people can recalibrate. Is that of understanding?

29. Hello ABE. We wish to clarify by asking our first question again - can you explain 'who' is ABE?

We are glad to come forth and clarify and we see that we have but already described what we are, but maybe a deeper knowing is of essence here? You see, we have to be careful as to not explain our way into thinking that you and we are of any indifference at all, not at core. We are but your original state of being, it is just that you do so have conditions of a body which creates different vibratory interference in a way. For you see, we do not have a physical body and are not of a point of place only, but when in communication with you both. The reason we are to come forth as ABE is because we are but a focal point of constricted consciousness shortened to become, or seem to become, separate - but we are not. You are just being receptive to this conscious flow and in this it has taken form in a sense through yourselves. See it as a radio station in which you would like to listen to. You tune in to certain channel, but you see you have but no preference and it is allowing more to come forth. Like we say, ABE is just a shortened constriction, of the whole thing - an abbreviation of pure consciousness. Is this of understanding now?

30. Is there anything ABE would wish to say to 'finalize' this book material - perhaps as an end message to the reader?

We would like to say that we are grateful for this communication and that there is always space and time, we are not in a great hurry. But we do so feel that this information is of importance now. People are the key connection, are the source, and unification is really what you are. You see, for something to become anything it starts with nothing; when all is seen that this is but the cycle of life then you could probably loosen up a little and allow all that you are to flow through you, unrestricted by what you have been conditioned to think, to be. The time is now to understand your extraordinary existence and at the same time your very ordinary existence - this is true unification of being. And you will see that you start to breathe again, you start to live again, and you start to love again. What a journey. You see, in this you realize you have come but full circle - but this time you are awake, you are alive. With much Love and Light - ABE.

PART THREE

Re-Connecting to Our Future

Chapter Thirteen

Re-unification

'The future enters into us…in order to transform itself in us long before it happens.'

Rainer Maria Rilke

As I have shown throughout this book, the world around – as well as our perception of it – is shifting dramatically. It feels as if something incredible is unfolding. What that 'something' is, is transforming itself through us, as the above quote from Rilke suggests. As a species, we are unfolding new faculties of perception. As these faculties continue to unfold, so too does our perspectives, and thus our relationship, to the grand reality in which human beings are embedded. New vistas are opening up, allowing humans to perceive fundamentally new insights upon the nature of reality, the cosmos, and their place in it. It is no exaggeration to say that humanity now stands at the crossroads of a new era. Where we go from here will dictate the future timeline for all those who shall come after.

Any new understanding needs to be arranged into coherency and comprehension, and into a vision that can be shared and comprehended by others. Humanity can gain incredible meaning from any new understanding gleamed of the cosmos and of their relation to it. However, we need to make it real for us. We must absorb and digest what the implications are for shifting our perspectives to align with the new view of life in a fundamentally interconnected and intelligent cosmos. Finally, to benefit from this knowledge and understanding, we shall need to apply it practically to our lives. If we cannot make tangible this new vision that has been gained, how can it truly benefit our lives?

At the beginning of this book I explained that humanity is on a long-standing quest for meaning. However, searching is only one part of the quest. The next step that comes is *living* it. If we are unable to integrate these new perceptions of life and reality, then what is the point? As an intelligent, sentient species, humankind is meant to adapt the new perspectives it gains into developing itself upon both an external as well as internal path.

We have now come to understand that reality, as we know it (materially and energetically), exists as a totally interdependent and unified whole of which we are a part. As our understanding of reality unfolds, so do *we* develop as human beings. Like a feedback loop, the more understanding we receive, the more it pushes forth our perceptions onto ever greater understanding. As this book has shown, all life exists as part of not only a participatory cosmos but also a sensitive cosmos – it is sensitive to our presence, participation, and projections. And the more that science delves into the structure of the cosmos, the more those structures reveal not only external forms of connectivity and correspondence but, more remarkably and importantly, an unseen yet underlying unified coherence. Just because a thing cannot be seen does not mean it does not exist. There is a metaphysical background to world reality that pushes through into the physical everyday world. What we can say about 'reality' is that it is a mix, a blend, of the tangible and the intangible.

The physical reality of the world can be described as unfolding from an unseen realm (the Unified Source Field). There is evidently more to cosmic reality than its physical manifestations. It is therefore only natural that, in response to this new understanding, human life should shift into greater correspondence with these perspectives. Should we not be applying these correspondences to manage relations between the tangible and the intangible to make the world a better place?

To use modern computer terminology, everything within the Unified Source Field is part of the same program. Every area of the program is intrinsically connected to every other part. Each component, or consciousness, also ultimately depends upon the other to retain the wholeness of the program. Collaboration and interconnectivity are thus the very basis of existence – energetically as well as materially. This can be called a form of mutual symmetry – a dance or exchange of energy and information that functions through coherence and resonance. These are values that form part of the understanding of living within a unified existence.

Values of a Unified Existence

Contemporary science has now come to recognize that all life exists as part of a nonlocally interconnected reality. As such, we are seeing features of this underlying reality manifesting into the physical world of our daily lives. One example of this is how social and human connectivity has shifted from hierarchical structures to decentralized and distributed networks. It can be recognized how these material shifts are corresponding to greater degrees of human interrelatedness. Recently, people have increasingly spoken of connection, communication, networking, and collaboration. These are the signifiers of an integrated, more holistic view of life.

Previously, I have written of how we are witnessing a transition from one set of 'C-Values' – **Competition ~ Conflict ~ Conquest ~ Control ~ Censorship** – toward a new set of 'C-Values' - **Connection ~ Communication ~ Collaboration ~ Consciousness ~ Compassion.**[37] At the core of existence is an energetic pattern of unity. As we come to grasp this sense of essential unification, perhaps this will have a knock-on effect on how people behave. That is, how we *do* things and the

· · · · · · · · · · · ·
37   These values were first put forth in my book *The Phoenix Generation: A New Era of Connection, Compassion & Consciousness* (2014)

way we do them. That is, outer circumstances will begin to reflect not only our inner realities but also the reality of the cosmos. This may sound like a tall order, as they say; yet, the greater is reflected in the smaller, and the smaller contains the seed of the greater. Or, to put it another way – 'As Above, So Below' – as the Hermetic maxim goes.

These correspondences are now coming more to the fore. Technology should not be something that is *beyond* or separate from people. Rather, technologies should be an extension of ourselves - a projection of our intention to interact and interface with the environment around us. Technologies tend to reflect the state of human consciousness. Some technologies may even arise in accordance with our state of readiness to understand them - they are a representation of ourselves and reveal human visions (and often our limitations!) The relationship between technologies with the state of human consciousness is often overlooked. Sometimes this innate relationship is out of balance, is lopsided and incongruous, and results in technologies of destruction (such as in warfare). Other times, the relationship is more aligned and results in creative innovation that aims toward the betterment of human life upon the planet.

Humanity has experienced a consciousness of acquisition, possession, ownership, and control for far too long. Many people, in developed nations at least, have been living with the gold rush for capitalism, consumerism, copyright, and control. It was all very tangible, and solid, and could be seen, felt, and known. Now we are seeing a break-up of these older models as newer social forms arise. We can only hope these will serve us better than our previous 'masters.' It does seem that human civilization is transforming toward lighter, more subtle, forms of connectivity and communion. And these are pushing human cultures toward newer forms of social relations.

Relations of a Unified Existence

The perspective from the Unified Source Field view is that Nature is not something separate from humans but rather that we are in communion with it. Nature, as already many sensible people know, is an inclusive part of all relations on this planet. And we must start from here – from our collective roots. External relations often take time to arrange and settle themselves into a more harmonious relationship. The importance of connection is to shift toward the greater importance of being relational. As ABE emphasized in their communications – our relations are everything, and we need to bring them back home to ourselves. Also, there are signs that a 'feminine' type of energy is entering more into global systems. Let me explain what I mean by this, as I am not speaking in terms of gender – but *energetic relations*.

It can be recognized that a 'feminine impulse' has been the energy behind the increased global interconnection and inter-relationality. The vastly expanding digital world is more than a communication device, more than an 'Inter-net;' rather, it is a mirroring of our own cosmic *Inner-net*. This transition to a more integrated society calls for a return to ecological values and relations. These are essential in how complex and decentralized networks need to recalibrate. New initiatives, innovations, projects, friendships and relations, are emerging from this interconnected ecology. The new multiplicities are undermining the once-dominant top-down hierarchical systems (which can be denoted as the 'masculine energy'). The new collaborative spaces are all about multitasking - from share economies to open-access information. Global platforms are increasingly becoming a place/space for such issues as human rights, education, health care, childcare, welfare, and the environment, etc. These mounting issues, as well as the manner of how they are multi-tasked and openly discussed, all belong to the unified field values of collaboration, connection, communication, consciousness, and compassion.

All these changes mark a shift to new models of exchange, away from ownership and toward access. That is, moving away from centralization into a world of flows and relations. This form of ecosystem is more open to be nourished from user-generated content, representing increased participation from people. These forms of relations more naturally facilitate individuation (rather than self-centered individualism) and the creation of new forms of community and belonging.

Access and use of an interconnected ecosystem of communication and relations can help in dissolving and breaking down social divisions. That is, individuals realize that they are empowered actors as part of an increasingly collaborative system. However, increased connectivity does not necessarily create immediate tolerance – not all changes in perspective and lifestyle will come easy. Yet it is almost certain that increased interconnectivity will have a great impact upon our societies, restructuring cultural norms and social behavior.

A different world is emerging – being birthed – and it needs to find its place. Values are shifting, new modes and ways of doing things are causing disruption, and many things – as well as many people – are on the move. Many aspects of our societies are shaking off the older energy relations and recalibrating for a new unified reality perception to unfold. It will not be a totally smooth process. There is a 'clash of ideologies-mythologies' occurring right now during this transition period. And yet greater instability is also a sign of incredible change on the horizon.

The inequalities and human brutalities that occur in the world largely stem from antiquated human thinking and the older values of greed, power, and control that represent the old paradigm system. No great technological marvel will alter these human traits – only a shift in human consciousness. And this is already occurring within each new generation coming into the world. The *reality shift* that is underway may not sit kindly, or easily, with many of the older minds of the older generations. Already many 'older minded' people are feeling overwhelmed by this sudden rush of change and recalibration. The newer generations are being born into a different cultural ecosystem that will feel natural to them, where old boundaries and frontiers have been rearranged. New cultural identities are emerging.

Identities of a Unified Existence

The new ecosystem of values and relations that is emerging is not only impacting *how* we do things but also *who* we are in this changing reality. The notion of human identity is experiencing further shifts in how people relate to their fellow humans, and how people understand themselves as part of a unified reality. Many people are now being forced to question their social identity as well as their role and future upon the planet. Debates concerning the quintessential features of human identity are set to become critical in the coming years - 'being human' will become a central, and for some, delicate subject.

The incoming phase of change that a shift in consciousness will bring to humanity will compel people to reconsider, and perhaps redefine, what it means to be human. The seeds for this were planted decades before, especially in the late twentieth-century. We are now being further compelled to deeply consider, perhaps through much soul-searching, what it means to be human. We are perhaps only now, especially during these turbulent years of radical social changes, beginning to consider how these emerging connections and relations are affecting our inner selves.

My sense is that people shall be stimulated into searching for greater meaning, purpose, and direction. We are already being urged to reflect and understand human life from outside all previous boxes of thought. Humanity is now stepping out of its' pre-programmed boxes of thinking into a new landscape.

Psychologists are already recognizing the rise of empathy across the world as many people – especially the younger generations - are forming expanded relations. There is an increased rise of relations with strangers, and empathy with those that are in difficulties or are experiencing challenging times. This sense of human solidarity, a feeling of compassion for others, is growing stronger within the minds and hearts of people as they feel naturally connected to those from beyond their localized communities. Identities are becoming more fluid as people recognize themselves as being planetary citizens rather than relating solely with national identities. New patterns will arise within human reality in terms of how people live, connect, communicate, collaborate, understand, produce, and create value and meaning in their lives.

The recognition that we live as part of an intelligent, conscious Unified Source Field is likely to make people feel even more special and privileged to be a human being. It will trigger humanity into developing new skills and creative ways of being that will shape a radically different human future.

Chapter Fourteen

Feeling Connected

'Who looks outside, dreams; who looks inside, awakes.'

Carl Gustav Jung

Human consciousness is going to go through an extraordinary transformation as it shifts to align with the new understandings and perspectives. It can be said that this new information, such as discussed in this book, will serve to give human perception a form of 'upgrade.' It would be fair to say that what is being experienced in these coming years is on a par with what occurred as human consciousness shifted from a 'flat earth' to a 'round earth' perspective. It was a turnabout that changed everything. It is no understatement to say that human life on this planet is on the cusp of a revolutionary shift in perception. And this shift shall mark everything that occurs afterwards. It is also my sense that this change in human perceptions will stimulate a turning toward greater inner reflection. One result of this shall be a strengthening in the recognition and expression of one's inner authority.

This recognition of a person's inner authority supports what is known as *instinctual intelligence* as compared to externally acquired knowledge. That is, rather than acting from acquired information (based on educational conditioning), people will increasingly turn to trusting an internal sense – their 'gut instinct,' as they say. Also, as each person learns to trust their inner instinct they are increasingly seeing through the fog of cultural conditioning. This is important to stress as much of the older and current thinking patterns have been generated through forms of conditioning. With an expansion in human perception, people are going to become increasingly aware of social and cultural propaganda. As such, people will be less susceptible to the manipulations inherent in the institutions of economics, politics, and health, for example. They should also be more able to recognize falsehoods and improprieties connected with religious doctrine and pseudo-spiritual teachings. The veil, I suspect, will begin to lift, similar to how Dorothy finally recognized that the roguish 'Wizard of Oz' was a projection from someone pulling the levers behind the curtain.

Many incumbent belief systems are likely to fall away as human consciousness starts to clear the fog of previous dominant thinking. One of these is the 'belief' that we are nothing more than a physical human being and that there are no other realms/dimensions beyond the earthly experience. This will lead to a reappraisal of ancient wisdom as people awaken to the potential for change that is within each of them. It will be a time for breaking the chains of the 'perception prison' that has bound humans for so long. Perhaps unknowingly, we became accustomed to living within limited perception-sets that over time became our prisons. These 'prisons' that hold us are the *cognitive systems* that we employ to interpret the world around. Part of what has been explored throughout this book will operate, in varying degrees, to 'bust' some of these dominant cognitive systems.

In order to move beyond the restrictions of current thinking, this book has suggested that not only is there is an intelligence behind the physical-material universe but also that this intelligence shows meaning and purpose. More importantly, that it is possible to gain access to this underlying intelligence and to learn from it – and that this can also give meaning and purpose. Under the right conditions, we can open a window between ourselves and this intelligence that pervades the cosmic reality. We can access its knowledge and information – it is gifted to us. Yet in our ordinary state, human perceptions (including the brain) are not equipped to decode this information or perceive this contact. We generally only decode, from the surrounding reality, that which is necessary, or deemed useful, for our immediate day-to-day life. This is largely because we are ignorant of the possibility for such communication. Yet it lies latent within all people, like an underused muscle. And like any normal muscle, it needs training to strengthen it. Each person can, likewise, strengthen their own muscles of communication and connection with this underlying conscious intelligence. It may not come in the direct form of an ABE - it may come through internal *nudges*, or intuitions, or that familiar voice at the back of the mind that has always spoken in whispers. Whether we care to admit it or not, we each know that there is a part 'of us' that speaks internally, apart from the regular thought patterns. It has always been that quiet voice within that we know we can trust, although perhaps seldom do we follow it. It seems that now, perhaps, this barrier, or veil, is thinning; that greater interaction and communication is set to occur between the individual and the larger consciousness field. Soon, we may all be able to consciously connect with the 'cloud' and download – or rather, gain – an increased wisdom and sense of *what to do* in our lives. And such knowledge must not only be integrated into our minds – the intellectual understanding - but also integrated into emotional and social being. Life is going to radically change in the years ahead. In fact, it has already begun to change.

Situations will continually arise that call into question many different aspects of our lives. Human beliefs, perceptions, and perspectives will be greatly challenged. How we choose to respond to this will impact our very principles and cherished values. Again, we are being asked to consider and reflect on *how* and *what* we think – and *why*. Humanity has now entered a momentous period of transition. At such times, the sides of the box fall away. And we should not be in such a rush to put the lid back on again. As shown in Part One, humanity exists as an interconnected organism – through field consciousness as well as through physical networks of shared, collective intelligence. These collective networks do not negate our individual agency; on the contrary, they show that we are fundamentally operating at a deeper level than many have ever suspected. The Jungian psychologist Marie-Louise von Franz commented that,

> 'Whenever an individual works on his own unconscious, he invisibly affects first the group and, if he goes even deeper, he affects the large national units or sometimes even all of humanity. Not only does he change and transform himself but he has an imperceptible impact on the unconscious psyche of many other people.'[38]

Similarly, Chris Bache's immersion into humanity's collective being (Chapter Six) gave him the realization that there were grander processes operating beneath the surface of individual lives that were weaving humanity into a larger whole. From these experiences, Bache came to recognize the 'living tissue' of the human species, affirming the existence and influence of the collective unconscious. Bache goes on to make a profound statement:

> '...consciousness is an open field and within this field, states of consciousness are contagious...Like ripples spreading across water, this is an utterly natural effect. When one person begins to throw off layers of their psychological conditioning and awaken to clearer, more expansive states of awareness, surrounding people will necessarily be affected. Our spiritual ecology simply does not permit private awakening. *The ecology of consciousness is an inherently collective ecology.*'[39]

• • • • • • • • • • • • •
38   Cited in Bache, Christopher M. 2019. *LSD & The Mind of the Universe*. Rochester, VT: Park Street Press, p137
39   Bache, Christopher M. 2019. *LSD & The Mind of the Universe*. Rochester, VT: Park Street Press, p199

We are each affected by the 'consciousness ripples' emanating from others. It is how the ecology of consciousness operates. And since it is an interconnected ecology, individual awakening – or expansion of awareness – does not just remain at the individual level. What we feed into our localized fields of consciousness will then go on to form part of a larger body, or consciousness field. And this, ultimately, will form part of a grander resonating field of collective consciousness – at the community, national, and global level. Psychologically, we are not alone. Each person lives as a part of the world, and not apart from it. Each person has a responsibility to manage their thoughts – what they receive and process as well as what they transmit. Therefore, *what* and *how* we think is indeed part of each person's responsibility. As Sri Aurobindo said – 'But now we have, very remarkably, very swiftly coming to the surface this new psychological tendency of the communal consciousness.'[40]

This 'communal consciousness' of increasing awareness will assist the human species in moving forward collectively. As each person individually develops their understanding and perception of the bigger picture, so will this 'awakening' spread further throughout the human collective consciousness. Yet these changes and shifts will not happen overnight. Like ink dots spreading across the blotting paper, they shall occur in phases until eventually the paper has crossed the tipping-point

• • • • • • • • • • • •
40   Aurobindo, S. (1999 [1950]). *The Human Cycle: The Psychology of Social Development*. Twin Lakes, WI, Lotus Light Publications, p38

and flipped into a new color. Whether we choose to manifest things in life, facilitate for others, or nurture others, human cooperation has shown to lead toward greater coherence as a whole.

Toward Planetary Coherence

A grand sweep of history shows the rise and fall not only of countless civilizations and empires, but also the shifts in human perceptions and consciousness. How we *see* the world, and our place in it, has always influenced how, and to what degree, we participate and create the human world we live within. Until very recently, the consensus had been to view the world as exterior to the human being – as separate and fragmented. These dominant modes of thinking brought forth much conflict and divisions. The energy for growth was sought from friction rather than coherence. Exclusion was more prominent than inclusion. Yet now, the human future requires a different *modus operandi;* from hereon, the fundamental energy of sustainable growth requires greater stability and coherence.

The age of one empire alone dominating the world is at an end. The present multi-polar world reflects a level of deep interconnectivity between the dominant, and also not-so-dominant, nations, states, and regional blocks. Paradoxically, however, this early stage of global interconnectivity and interdependence is creating conflict amongst the major players – the very opposite of what we would expect to see in a drive toward coherence. So, where is the underlying coherence behind this display of social disruption?

My own perspective is that coherence is emerging from the bottom up, through the ecosystem of individual consciousnesses across the planet, rather than from the top-down structures. Humanity is a vehicle, a channel, for *extending mind* across the Earth. In other words, human beings are embracing the planet like a membrane, a living skin. Just as the skin is the largest organ of the human body, the *living skin* of the planet shall come through the shifts towards greater connectivity and communion in consciousness. The increasing awareness of the interconnection between humanity and the larger cosmos serves as a driver toward further coherence. Again, how we *see* the world also influences how we participate and create the world for human living.

The rise of greater communion, coherence, and hence stability across the planet will first have to emerge through the individual consciousnesses of the people. It will spread through entangled fields of consciousness as well as through the expanding interconnected technological networks. The impulse behind the new future paradigm will facilitate greater integration between matter (tangible) and consciousness (intangible). Just as computer systems use the binary code of 0s and 1s to form a communicative whole, so does this reflect the entanglement of the tangible (1) with the intangible (0).

The world that humans experience reflects a grander, underlying, unified reality. As human beings, we each interact with the world differently because we *perceive* the world differently. In interacting differently, we each contribute to creating a participatory world. Knowledge, and recognition, of the Unified Source Field, and of its conscious intelligence, infuses the human condition with a new vista of reality. In no way does it detract from the meaning and purpose of being human. On the contrary, it adds to it - as I discuss in the remaining chapters. To be a human being is to be inherently imbued with a life force that animates the person in ways we are largely unaware of. Through this animated force we perceive the surrounding world, and from this we cultivate our worldview and values. And a civilization's worldview is its most precious possession.

It is recognized that human understanding is developed within specific cultural environments. Our ancestors responded to a different world and so developed a different world view. In each time, in each epoch, we articulate the human condition within a different dimension of awareness. We articulate the essence of the human condition according to our times. It is now the time to articulate the human condition according to the understanding of a unified, intelligent cosmos. I personally believe we have the capacity to respond likewise intelligently to this knowledge, and from this to unfold a new vision of the cosmos and of reality. And this is to be a vision that is more relevant and useful to the current times. From this perspective, we may see the world return to be an exciting, magical, and mysterious domain once again. The world is reviving its sense of being a *Misterium Tremendes*, a sacred place to dwell in.

As a transformation in human awareness unfolds, we shall not only be changing the ways we think but also the ways we *do* things. We will learn how to be present in a world where we are receiving, holding, and transmitting consciousness upon various levels. It will benefit people to know that an intelligent, creative, and nurturing energy is flowing *through* them in so many ways - the appreciative touch, the supportive word, the reassuring glance that we each can weave into our lives. This is part of a *living soul* that comes through a collective species body. As Meister Eckhart said – 'The soul is not in the body; the body is in the soul.'

Such a connected life is already affecting many people, influencing thinking patterns and consciousness whether the person is aware of it or not. Our perspectives on the world and the cosmos have been changing dramatically over recent years. Many people, perhaps a majority now, have already come to the realization that we do not exist as part of a dead universe. We are slowly metamorphosing out of our cocoon of cosmic quarantine. The recognition that the human being is a significant part of an enchanted cosmos is growing. The innate state of humanity is to feel integral to all life. This too provides for the integrity and stability of the human psyche. This continuity has only been disrupted for a time – become fragmented. As ABE said, we forgot to get back on the phone line again. Yet the line was never disconnected. It remains open, waiting for us to remember and pick it back up again. And that time is now. It is time to return to a re-connection with a source of meaning.

As we reconnect again, we each can bring a spark into the burning flame of the species *living soul*. This is already happening through the ever-increasing numbers of people who are awakening to their new perspectives on life. And this shall usher in a new human era. As the Indian sage Sri Aurobindo said,

> The coming of a spiritual age must be preceded by the appearance of an increasing number of individuals who are no longer satisfied with the normal intellectual, vital and physical existence of man, but perceive that a greater evolution is the real goal of humanity and attempt to effect it in themselves, to lead others to it and to make it the recognized goal of the race.'[41]

The integration of the inner world of the individual with their external world can bring greater cohesion, stability, and meaning into life. After all, our lives must have meaning for us individually before we can bring authentic meaning into the lives of others.

To some degree, our far human ancestors were aware that they lived as part of an integral, unified cosmos where the material, tangible worlds existed alongside the energetic, intangible worlds. This worldview is one that accepts not only the metaphysical but also the magical and the mysterious. As human awareness expands, we will become more intelligible to ourselves, and become capable of recognizing the truer nature of the cosmos and reality. And this shall bring greater purpose and meaning to our lives.

• • • • • • • • • • • •
41   Aurobindo, Sri (1999/1950) *The Human Cycle: The Psychology of Social Development.* Twin Lakes, WI, Lotus Light Publications, p263

Chapter Fifteen
Shifting Perceptions

'You must prepare yourself for the transition in which there will be none of the things to which you have accustomed yourself.'

Al-Ghazali

Al-Ghazali, the 11th century philosopher, compares the effect of being cut-off from humanity's natural connection with Source as being likened to a deprivation of food or certain medicines. The skills that preserve this connection he refers to as 'special knowledge' – 'The "special knowledge" is that which supports life to such an extent that if its transmission were to be interrupted for three days the kernel of the individual dies, just as someone would die if he were deprived of food, or a patient dies when deprived of certain medicines.'[42] This was ancient knowledge, now almost forgotten or thrown away from modern perspectives. Yet it is the state of the human mind and perception that

· · · · · · · · · · · ·
42   Shah, Idries, (1971) *Thinkers of the East*. London: Jonathan Cape, p177

drives history and the welfare and evolution of civilizations.

The perspectives we hold as an individual, a culture, a species, reflects our state of consciousness and access to knowledge. For far too long, humanity has considered itself separate from the cosmos. As Jung once remarked, the human feels as if exiled and cosmically isolated. That was also why Jung stated that the human being does not know themselves. It is a paradox perhaps that the human being does not fully know itself and yet the long journey of our species history is also the story of human agency. As a species, we've experienced the growth of conscious awareness over millennia, with its expression through many and varied teachings and philosophies (including religions). These stages in human thinking all influenced our understanding of individuality, identity, and the human condition. And yet, despite all the novel forms of thinking and expressions of human consciousness, we still lack a coherent, civilizing cosmology. Perhaps our all too well-known history of human separation is now beginning to be replaced by a consciousness of connection and communion? In other words, humanity is moving into greater empathic connection with a living cosmos. The messages from ABE are a reminder that the only real place we need to get to is Home - there is nowhere else to go when the cosmos already exists within the human being.

The more individuals that connect across the expanding planetary networks, the greater will be the perception of our species interconnectivity. It will be easier to accept our inherent connection with the cosmic source field if we can first manifest a species field connectivity. This is emerging now, manifesting through the physical-digital networks that connect people across the world. Whether the individual fully realizes this or not, there is a hyper-connectivity within the human species field. A collective psyche is in formation. We may perceive this currently as temporary fluctuations – a whole range of news, ideas, opinions, fears, anxieties, hopes, and urges spread through the global psyche. Yet this is just one stage within humanity's long journey toward self-activated collective awareness. At some point, these fluctuations will settle to form a permanent psychological state. In the words of Chris Bache:

> ...under the pressure of the extreme conditions of our future, the human psyche will come alive at new levels, that something like psychological phase-locking will take place, that the interconnections between people previously too subtle to be detected will become obvious, and that all of this will take place much faster than anyone could have predicted.[43]

What Bache recognizes, and to which I concur, is that what appear to be the crises in the global systems externally are deeply connected to the shifts in consciousness taking place within the collective psyche of humanity. The global struggles to become increasingly interconnected reflect the shifts to become more psychologically integrated

43   Bache, Christopher M. 2019. *LSD & The Mind of the Universe*. Rochester, VT: Park Street Press, p227

as a species. As individuals, we represent the expression of nonlocal consciousness, and its potential to empower through local manifestation. And as both individuals and a collective species, we are constantly evolving.

The present stage of humanity is not permanent – it is transitional. Forms in transition often reach pivotal moments. These are known in the sciences as *bifurcation points*.[44] At such moments, an energetic-chaotic system either pushes through to a new level of arrangement – or it breaks down. What is evident now is that as individuals we are cells within a superorganism that is in the throes of a transitional shift to a new arrangement of life. Such moments of great transition are seldom comfortable. The period of discomfort is part of the healing process. Transition can be seen as a period of detoxification whereby certain psychological aspects – such as old paradigm perceptions and related behaviors – are pushed to align with newer necessities. Again, I refer to transpersonal researcher Chris Bache who, in a series of later transcendental sessions, was given the following visions:

> *When an organism is called on from within to become more conscious, it must first cleanse itself of the psychological by-products of living at its lower level of awareness. It must bring forward the residue of its past and purge that residue from its system in order to lay*

· · · · · · · · · · · · ·
44   See - Laszlo, Ervin (2006) *The Chaos Point: The World at the Crossroads.* Charlottesville, VA: Hampton Roads.

*the foundation for a more refined level
of operation...I saw that the generations
born in our period of history had been
deliberately configured to precipitate an
intense cycle of collective purification.
The poisons of humanity's past were
being brought to the surface in us, and
by us transforming these poisons in our
individual lives, we were making it possible
for divine awareness to enter more deeply
into future generations.'[45]*

Bache's visions continued to show him a tipping-
point into a new world emergence:

*Amidst a field of relative calm, a small
anxiety began to grow. Slowly more and
more persons were looking up and becoming
alarmed. Like persons living on an island
(before modern weather forecasting) who
gradually became aware that a hurricane is
overtaking them, humanity was gradually
waking up with alarm to events that had
overtaken it. Conditions got worse and
worse. People became more and more
alarmed as the danger increased, forcing
them to let go of their assumptions at deeper
and deeper levels. The world as they knew
it was falling apart...Everywhere new
social institutions sprang into being that
reflected our new reality - new ways of
thinking, new values that we had discovered
within ourselves during the crisis. Every
aspect of our lives was marked by new
priorities, new perceptions of the good, new*

truths. These new social forms reflected new states of awareness that seemed to spread through the survivors like a positive contagion. These social forms then fed back into the system to elicit still newer states of awareness in individuals, and the cycle of creativity between individual and group spiralled.'[46]

From these visions Bache came to believe that humanity is coming into what he refers to as a time of 'Great Awakening.' That is, Bache envisions a profound shift in the fundamental condition of the human psyche occurring in these times. I described this in an earlier book where I put forth that the world is undergoing three types of revolution, all co-dependent: physical, psychic and cosmological. [47] I spoke about how, as a collective species, we are going to go through a 'Dark Night of the Soul' moment - a collective death and re-awakening akin to the Hero's Journey.[48] As Bache likewise foresees, such an awakening must by necessity be preceded by a 'Great Death' – or period of transition whereby the old systems must be cleansed or removed in order to make way for the new. It will be a period of discomfort, of anxiety and anguish, in order for a new formation of the human being and human society to emerge. Bache declares that: 'I believe that through the global systems crisis, our planet is giving birth to the Future Human.'[49]

• • • • • • • • • • • • •
46   Ibid., p222-3
47   Dennis, Kingsley (2012) *New Revolutions for a Small Planet.* London: Watkins Publishing.
48   See - https://en.wikipedia.org/wiki/Hero%27s_journey
49   Bache, Christopher M. 2019, p209

The interim transition period can be viewed from a perspective that sees it as a collective detoxification and healing. The collective human psyche is flushing out its past toxins so as to lay the foundation for a wonderfully new future. This is also reflected in part by what ABE sees as *The Way Back Home*. In Chapter Ten, the question was asked to ABE - **Are we going to experience a period of increased disruption?** ABE replied:

We would like to say that these vibrations and energies are manifesting at great intensity and there will be ones that fight hand and tooth to keep things the way they are now. You see, when the seed is cracked open it could be seen as completely destructive, when in essence it is bringing new life. For the new life to come forth, the old shell that contained this new life will have to crack open and this will be extremely destructive. For the more this energy is brought forth, or we prefer 'allowed,' you are tapping it in and grounding it down into this reality. In this, it will shake away all that has been built, and in this you will see that the ones who cannot walk this path will not be able to succeed…To answer if there is increased disruption, we would say yes; as there are many that are grounding this vibration. They are unifying this of us and that of you, so the more people do this the more it will be destructive for the systems in place now. When you see more disruption, you will know that more people are enabling unification. ABE.

The crack in the seed may seem destructive, as ABE says, yet it is the form in which to bring new life forth. Disruptions are the 'strange attractors' that can pull humanity toward its future. We should not repel such times of discomfort – 'fight hand and tooth to keep things the way they are' – but allow this new energy to unfold. The time of this human transition has been envisioned by many others too.

In an interview with the notable monk and yogi Bede Griffiths, only months before his death, Andrew Harvey was given this unexpected dialogue:

> Bede paused suddenly (we had been talking about his early love of the romantic poets) and then said, quietly and intensely, "you know, of course, Andrew, that we are now in the hour of God."
>
> Although it was a warm, fragrant morning, I shivered.
>
> "When you say 'hour of God,' what do you mean?"
>
> "I mean that the whole human race has now come to the moment when everything is at stake, when a vast shift of consciousness will have to take place on a massive scale in all societies and religions for the world to survive. Unless human life becomes centered on the awareness of a transcendent reality that embraces all humanity and the whole universe and at the same time transcends our present level of life and consciousness, there is little hope for us...Very few people are prepared to look without illusion at our time and see it for what it is—a crucifixion on a worldwide scale of everything humanity has expected or trusted or believed in every level and in every arena. To look

like this requires a kind of final faith and courage, which few have as yet. You and others like you will have to live and write in such a way as to help people to such a faith and trust."

… We sat together in silence, absorbing the pain and challenge of his words. Then I asked, "Do you think humanity can get through?"

"Of course," he said immediately, his voice strong, "but it will cost everything. Just as Jesus had to go through death into the new world of the Resurrection, so millions of us will have to go through a death to the past and to all old ways of being and doing if we are going to be brought by the grace of God into the truth of a real new age. The next twenty years will unfold a series of terrible disasters, wars, and ordeals of every kind that will reveal if the human race is ready to die into new life or not. I have no idea of what the outcome of the savage period we are entering will be. There are many prophecies in many mystical traditions that speak of the horror of this time, but they disagree as to what will happen. This I think shows that either total destruction or total transformation is possible and depend on us, on what we choose, and how we act." [50]

How we act will depend upon the perceptions and perspectives we choose to adopt. The states of consciousness we are each open to results from the responsibility of our choices. As ABE has shown in their previous messages, we are all a part of a unified

· · · · · · · · · · · ·
50   Andrew Harvey, 'Servant of a Transformed Future: A Meeting with Bede Griffiths' - http://www.alternativesmagazine.com/33/harvey.html

reality. We have always been in conversation with ourselves – just that most of us, most of the time, didn't know it. The 'way back home' is not one of distance – it is becoming who we already truly are. The purpose of 'awakening' is not to go anywhere – neither *higher* nor *further* – but to be more completely who we are within this physical reality. Awakening is not a form of escape to somewhere but rather an awareness of our greater participation within a shared unified existence.

Thomas Berry, in his book *The Great Work*, stated that we are now experiencing a moment of significance far beyond what any of us can imagine. Berry firmly believed that the 'mission of our times' is to reinvent the human. This is no small task. We have not done this before. We have little past experience to help steer this great endeavour. We are a human becoming – we must learn to become by experience. Our human future awaits us.

Chapter Sixteen
Our Human Future

*'We are the eyes through which the universe
contemplates itself.'*

Henryk Skolimowski

As human beings, we have great responsibility. We are not mere physical beings living out a lowly existence, below a great, expansive cosmic reality. This is a self-deception. And sometimes we are the worst perpetrators for deceiving ourselves. As I hope the reading of this book has shown, we are all participants and a relational part of a wondrous creative cosmic intelligence that is beyond words. Yet it is not beyond us – we are an integrated whole.

As human beings living a physical existence, we are the point of place for the collective consciousness field to be expressed into material manifestation. That is, immaterial consciousness (creative energy-information) can be merged with the material plane. As individuals, we can act as agents to express localized aspects of consciousness from the Unified Source Field. And this, perhaps, is part of our purpose as physical beings upon this planet. This 'local agency' can further be enhanced as each person becomes more aware of this potentiality – conscious awareness thus actualizing greater influence. There is hope that this represents a shift towards an increase in globally conscious individuals who are aware of the responsibilities of being interconnected with others.

We can no longer afford to continue as selfish individuals or an inarticulate mass. It is time to take up the mantle of having agency as aware individuals who seek to consciously connect, collaborate, and care about the future. Each and every person – as aspects of localized consciousness – reflect not only the greater Unified Source Field but, just as importantly, we are also a reflection of each other. As such, no individual lives within a shell, separated from everybody else, but is connected to all by both a tangible and intangible communion. And this reality reflects our true humanity. As we connect and share our collective thoughts, ideas, visions, etc., we shall be helping to strengthen the signal of a coherent species consciousness. A planetary consciousness, as expressed through a sentient, individualized humanity, may not only be a real possibility – it may very well be a fundamental cosmic purpose.

Our Human Purpose

I have discussed how the latest science suggests that our known reality is coded from a Unified Source Field beyond spacetime. This view proposes that the totality of this reality is *in-formed* from a deep consciousness beyond it. The known cosmos exists as a whole, integrated consciousness field, of which sentient life are localized manifestations. Various sacred texts and traditions have stated that the universe (material reality) came into being as a way for its Source 'to know itself' – "*I was a hidden treasure and wanted to be known*" (sacred hadith). This is reminiscent of *Know Thyself*, the famous maxim from the Delphi oracle. Or, as in the words of philosopher Henryk Skolimowski – 'We are the eyes through which the universe contemplates itself…We are cosmologizing the human.'[51] Self-reflection is one of the prized attributes of self-consciousness – yet how can the whole reflect upon itself?

Self-realization is something we credit to each attained individual consciousness; it is a path in which purpose and meaning are core drivers and potentials. I propose that human beings are naturally driven by a longing, a purpose; this signifies a connection, a communion, with a larger source beyond the individual. It is not a question of *ascending*, as this signifies a leaving, an escape from; rather, it is a question of *transcending* – of reaching for connection that is beyond the physical self while still in the physical. And this connection to a 'source' beyond oneself increases a person's sense of inner *knowing*, which they are then more liable to act upon. If more people were to act upon their inner knowing, we can only imagine what forms of social cohesion and advancement would emerge as a result of this.

. . . .
51   Skolimowski, Henryk (1994) *The Participatory Mind: A New Theory of Knowledge and of the Universe*. London, Penguin/Arkana, p3

To repeat, human consciousness is a localized expression of a greater unified consciousness that ultimately is Source. As individuals, we are animated by access to this greater consciousness field, which is then manifested through our creative expressions such as human societies and cultures. To put it another way, we are all localized reflections of a grander, unified Reality. The greater our individual perceptions and conscious realizations, the stronger is the connection to accessing Source. In turn, the Unified Source Field is likewise 'in-formed' through the emerging awareness of each of its conscious sub-parts. The art of living is that we each have a role in bringing the unfinished world into completion. Through our daily lives, we each cooperate in bringing the world into existence.

If enough localized consciousnesses were to develop further their intuitive knowing and conscious awareness, this would likely stimulate a planetary consciousness field to *in-form*. In this, we are each a conscious agent of cosmic realization and immanence. Each person has a role to play on this planet by raising their individual, localized expressions of consciousness. In doing so, each person can influence and inspire others in their lives to raise theirs, as well as reflecting back their conscious awareness into Source. In this way, each human being acts as both 'cosmic conscious agents' of Source as well as caretakers for their own planetary development.

Reality is not a static state but an active, fluid energetic realm that responds to conscious participation. It makes demands on us as we make our demands upon it. Having human purpose means realizing our creative contribution to reality and our connection to the grander unified whole that in-forms us. Humans have intrinsic purpose in recognizing themselves as expressions of a living cosmos. We can restore the natural harmony and communion of existence by reciprocating this multiple-flowing, open communication.

An individual can achieve this reciprocation through small acts of conscious participation. The social and cultural changes currently occurring across the planet may well be part of this process. Some things first need to come apart in order to recalibrate again with a more aligned energy. Let us not forget that all human expression is a form of integrated energy and intelligence; and with each advance we move a step closer to communion with the Unified Source Field. One day we may witness a grand awakening of a collective expression of consciousness upon the Earth – and this may very well be the purpose for sentient life. This is likely to be more reality than fantasy. The hidden treasure that is at the very core of our existence wishes to be known - for *us* to be known – by our individual journeys of self-realization. We are not alone – a great planetary future awaits us. Knowing this brings immense meaning and significance to living life in human form.

Our Human Meaning

Living as part of the Unified Source Field brings new meaning to the sense of wholeness and integration. Wholeness now means knowing that we are part of everything. We are *in* everything and everything is *within* us. Feelings of belonging, connection, and communion – with others, with our environment, and with the cosmos – comes from this understanding of the grander reality. If we accept that all existence is part of a Unified Source Field, then everywhere is sacred. There is no separation; there is no place that is not part of the unified field at all times. Your own backyard – right where you are sitting now – can be treated as sacred and in communion. Each person can tap into this source of energy, of inspiration, from any location. Since we exist in unity, the essential connection is everywhere, and always available.

Living in the Unified Source Field is first and foremost a knowing, and then a deep acceptance, that everything exists as part of a unity. To nurture and sustain this understanding gives immense meaning and gratitude to our lives.

We can each cultivate this awareness by reflecting upon the following points:

- All existence is a unity. This unity manifests both through essence and through form. In our earthly existence we are in form. Yet at all times each physical entity, and this includes the human being, is in-touch with a formless unity. A person may only *feel* disconnected from this greater reality. Remembrance and recognition can always activate a conscious connection throughout our daily lives.

- Unity may appear as fragmentation in the physical world. This is how senses perceive effects. Just as when light hits the water it appears to be deflected at an angle. The fundamental unity is likewise deflected by the medium of physical matter. Yet this is not so. Do not be deceived by the bodily senses – feel and intuit the inner communion.

- Love has traditionally been associated with intimate associates, family, and close friends. Genuine love is unconditional, and this reflects living in the unified field. This love can be extended to strangers across the other side of the planet. We can love differently, yet at its core the love vibration is essentially the same. By engaging in open-hearted connection and communication with others we will realize that we share unity through love.

- Humans have flaws. This is a part of our natural existence and what also makes us so wonderful. All flaws create a unity. Do not look at flaws and see them as cracks. See flaws as part of the stitches that hold together a greater, unified tapestry.

- Enlightenment is not about reaching a 'higher' place at all. People struggle because they feel they need to reach another place. Every place is here. It is a splintered mind that creates these separations. A person needs not be in any other place but here, where you are. Feeling the unity is not 'beyond' or 'higher' – it is where you are sitting right now. You don't need to get to anywhere – you only need to Be.

- Living in the Unified Source Field means there are no spaces of emptiness. There are no holes or gaps, other than the ones we create for ourselves. Fragmentation is a human creation and does not form part of the greater reality.

- Aligning to the Unified Source Field is about being receptive to flow. Flows create harmony and balance. It is important to allow oneself to open up to the flows. Don't try to struggle against what makes you uncertain. Some of the best opportunities come from unexpected areas. Allow these moments to arrive by accepting that things may flow in ways you do not initially understand. Wait, be patient – do not try to immediately block every unknown event in your life.

- To align with the Unified Source Field means it is important to cultivate balance. Things that may be good for you should not be focused on exclusively at the exclusion of other things. For example, you may wish to be a vegetarian, yet if this is not balanced by a healthy lifestyle overall then still there can be imbalance. Do not consider things in isolation but as part of a grander web of balance and correspondence.

- It's okay to allow some of the excessive baggage to fall away. Possessions are often those things that own us. Possessions are not only material objects; they can also be thoughts, grievances, desires, frustrations, etc. Every now and again we need to do a spring-clean upon ourselves and take out the excessive and unneeded baggage. Recognizing the unity is also about recognizing one's own inherent freedom – physically, mentally, and emotionally.

- Try not to be in total control of everything – no-one is in total control. That is only a cultural myth. Unexpected things will happen in a human life – let them occur. Be flexible. Bend in the wind like a willow tree. To bring things into harmony and balance is often more important than to bring things under control.

- Physical exercise is beneficial, yet no one practice is better than another. For example, yoga is no better than walking if you don't feel comfortable in yoga positions. Don't push yourself, or your body, into places that don't resonate with you. Feel what exercise works for you and take it steady. Don't be extreme – be joyful.

- You don't necessarily need to reach a 'higher' state or achieve this or that, or be better, be first, etc. You only need to remember that you have the connection with the unified whole within you. It is almost like being connected by phone. If you feel you need that connection again, pick up the phone and return the call.

- We often get lost in our ways of naming this, defining that, separating one thing from another. These are human-created traits. It is useful to classify things in life because the external world needs these definitions. Yet life does not need disunity – keep the energy unified within.

- Living in the Unified Source Field is about finding your truth. This comes from intuition and 'gut feeling.' It also comes from listening to the silent voice that speaks within you. Practice listening to this silent voice. Learn to know its feel, its texture, its resonance. Try following it more often. Learn to trust it.

- When we are about to think, or speak, in terms of 'either/or' try replacing this with 'and' and observe how the process, or situation, changes. Living within unity recognizes that inclusivity is a reflection of the greater unified whole.

- Living within unity is about manifesting coherence in our lives. To assist this, we must drop our fears. Fears over identity, status, of 'losing our personality,' are especially dominant blockages. Fear causes our receptivity to shrivel up. Allowing the flow means we observe the roots of our fears and let them go.

- We have been programmed as social creatures to believe that we are separate human beings living as separate objects in a 'live or die' world where we need to struggle 'tooth and claw' to survive. We have just been badly programmed, and we are not to blame. It takes time to de-program the conditioning. Allow this to happen gently. Treat yourself with patience and observe as these conditioned layers fall away. Say goodbye to the human machine.

- Identifying with one's country, or community, or team can be a positive identifier. Yet if this shifts into competition for superiority – i.e., 'mine' is better than 'yours' then we foster separateness and fragmentation. To resonate with the Unified Source Field, we need to shift from feelings of superiority to feelings of unity.

- Coherence and the drive towards wholeness are embraced by the values we align ourselves with. Try to remember, in everyday life, that the 'C Values' of connection, communication, collaboration, consciousness, and compassion will always create greater receptivity than the old-paradigm 'C Values' of competition, conflict, control, conquest, and censorship.

By recognizing the Unified Source Field, we learn that as we increase our awareness, understanding, and perceptions, we correspondingly develop our connection with this intangible dimension of reality. As we enter the third decade of the twenty-first century, humanity is experiencing a revolution in so many areas of life – socially, culturally, politically, technologically, and more. We have entered a period of profound revolutionary change. As a species, we are moving from the heavier energies of physical objects to the more ethereal quality of lighter energies, connections, and aspects of consciousness.

Living in the Unified Source Field is not only about how we learn to navigate through new and emerging energetic spaces but also, significantly, how we adapt to an expanding awareness in human perceptions. We are moving through a major scientific, psychological, social - and hence spiritual - shift as a species. This knowing brings also great responsibility.

There is little training available for such profound shifts underway in human perceptions and consciousness. Such a transition may indeed be unprecedented in the history of the human species. From the mouths of caves to the starry dynamo of the intelligent cosmos. It is a wondrous journey that lies ahead. New horizons are unfolding in each moment, within each breath. As a human family, we are bound to travel upon this journey together. We are connected. We are reflections of each other. We are One. Above all, it is wondrous.

It is our moment now to ALLOW.

Kingsley L. Dennis, PhD, is a full-time writer and researcher. He is the author of over fifteen books including *Hijacking Reality: The Reprogramming & Reorganization of Human Life*; *Healing the Wounded Mind*; *The Modern Seeker: A Perennial Psychology for Contemporary Times*; *The Sacred Revival*; *The Phoenix Generation*; *New Consciousness for a New World*; *Struggle for Your Mind*; and the celebrated *Dawn of the Akashic Age* (with Ervin Laszlo). Kingsley is the author of numerous articles on social futures, new technologies, and conscious evolution. He also writes books for young adults and other novels. Kingsley runs his own publishing imprint, Beautiful Traitor Books – www.beautifultraitorbooks.com. For more information, visit his website: www.kingsleydennis.com.

Nicola Mortimer is a mother of four creative children, owner of nothing in Leicestershire. She has had so many jobs she can't recall them all. She pursued a philosophy degree in hope to find answers to the BIG questions in life but quit the course to allow the answers to reveal themselves through BEING in life, the way she is. She had her initial connection with Abe in 2007 when she started to write bits amid her life questioning and asking, 'Is this what it's all about?' Yet Nicola did not fully accept the incoming nudges from Abe until around 2015 when she began to record her questions and answers. Nicola remains a lifelong questioner, seeker, and explorer of life's mysteries. She is also very, very normal.

---

*"The reason to communicate with you is
because of again resonance."*

The ABE materials are positive and
inspiring communications that urge
us to find our way back into balance
– from a 'splintered mind' into 'home
resonance.' These communications
are not a channeling but an allowing.
That is, each person has the potential
to connect with their origin, if they
allow the flow. ABE is you and me.
As ABE would say – 'there is no differing.'

We offer these communications in the
hope that they may be of benefit to
others – and to help as many as possible to find the way back home.

---

https://www.thewaybackhome.one

Beautiful Traitor Books was founded in 2012 as an independent print-on-demand imprint to provide unusual and inspiring books for the discerning reader.

Our books are works that delve into various domains whether it is books for children, science fiction, social affairs, philosophy, theatre plays, or poetry. We have books translated into Spanish, French, Portuguese, Italian, and Hungarian. All the books we publish seek to explore innovative and creative ideas. Many of them also tell a good story - stories that have different perspectives on life and on the human condition.

Beautiful Traitor Books is not only about offering the reader entertainment. We also seek to offer something that is like a nutrition; something of value that the reader can take away from the book. Good books function on more than one level. Put simply, we thrive on books that have the capacity to *shift* the reader.

Come and join the conversation – find out more at:
www.beautifultraitorbooks.com

Books deserving…

for inquiring minds…

CPSIA information can be obtained
at www.ICGtesting.com
Printed in the USA
BVHW091948280621
610637BV00003B/343